ELEMENTS OF COST-BENEFIT ANALYSIS

ELEMENTS OF
COST-BENEFIT ANALYSIS

BY

E. J. MISHAN

London

GEORGE ALLEN AND UNWIN

Boston   *Sydney*

First published in 1972
Second impression 1974
Second edition 1976
Second impression 1978

GEORGE ALLEN & UNWIN LTD

40 Museum Street, London WC1A 1LU

© George Allen & Unwin (Publishers) Ltd, 1972, 1976

ISBN   0 04 300035 5 *hardback*
0 04 300066 5 *paperback*

Printed in Great Britain by
Unwin Brothers Limited, The Gresham Press, Old Woking, Surrey

PREFACE

This volume offers an introduction to the logic of, and the concepts used in, cost-benefit analysis, one that is suitable for undergraduate students of economics and, indeed, accessible to anyone having some acquaintance with the elements of economics. No mathematical background is required of the reader, although a superficial knowledge of the more familiar diagrams used in economics may ease his passage through some parts of the book.

The final section on Uncertainty may be thought too brief even in an elementary treatise. But it is a peculiarly difficult aspect of the subject to deal with satisfactorily. In my larger book (*Cost-Benefit Analysis*) I have touched on the techniques associated with the development of decision theory – conditional probability, game theory, and utility theory – while observing that, as yet, such techniques are not much favoured in cost-benefit calculations; at least not for dealing with the uncertainty attaching to the magnitude of future prices and quantities of the expected stream of inputs and outputs. In the circumstances, I have chosen to restrict the treatment here to an outline of two quite practicable methods of dealing with the problem. Where public investment is large and continuous, the adoption of an appropriate discount rate is a valid way of coping with such uncertainty. Where, in contrast, public investment is not large, a distribution table constructed from subjective probabilities offers an easy and fairly effective way of coping with the problem.

The accent throughout this volume is on the basic ideas, on the rationale of cost-benefit analysis, on what is to count and what is not to count, rather than on the specific techniques used for estimating the relevant magnitudes. For this reason the treatment may also have some value for those engineers and statisticians who are called upon from time to time to contribute to the evaluation of a project, and who may occasionally feel a little unsure of the appropriate criterion or of the economic relevance of some of the items to be included as costs or benefits.

London, June 1971   *E.J.M.*

CONTENTS

PART I. INTRODUCTORY

CHAPTER 1

Why Cost-Benefit Analysis?

1. The general question that a cost-benefit analysis sets out to answer is whether a number of investment projects, *A, B, C,* etc., should be undertaken and, if investible funds are limited, which one two, or more, among these specific projects that would otherwise qualify for admission, should be selected. Another question to which cost-benefit analysis sometimes addresses itself is that of determining the level at which a plant should operate or the combination of outputs it should produce. In this introductory volume, however, we follow custom in confining our attention chiefly to the former question, about the choice of investment projects.

But why bother with cost-benefit analysis at all? What is wrong with deciding whether or not to undertake any specific investment, or to choose among a number of specific investment opportunities, guided simply by proper accounting practices and, therefore, guided ultimately by reference to profitability. The answer is provided by the familiar thesis that what counts as a benefit or a loss to one part of the economy – to one or more persons or groups – does not necessarily count as a benefit or loss to the economy as a whole. And in cost-benefit analysis we are concerned with the economy as a whole, with the welfare of a defined society, and not any smaller part of it.

A private enterprise, or even a public enterprise, comprises only a segment of the economy, often a very small segment. More important, whatever the means it employs in pursuing its objectives – whether rules of thumb or more formalized techniques such as mathematical programming or operations research – the private enterprise, at least, is guided by ordinary commercial criteria that require revenues to exceed costs. The fact that its activities are guided by the profit motive, however, is not to deny that it confers benefits on a large number of people other than its shareholders. It also confers benefits on its employees, on consumers, and – through the taxes it pays – on the general public. Yet the benefits enjoyed by these four groups continue to exist only for as long as they coincide with the yielding of profits to the enterprise. If it makes losses the enterprise cannot survive unless it receives a public subsidy. If it is to survive unaided as a private concern and, moreover, to expand the scale of its operations it must, over a period of time, produce profits large enough either to attract investors or to finance its own. expansion.

There is, of course, the metaphor of the 'invisible hand', the *deus ex machina* discovered by Adam Smith that so directs the self-seeking proclivities of the business world that it confers benefits on society as a whole. And one can, indeed, lay down simple and sufficient conditions under which the uncompromising pursuit of profits acts always to serve the public interest. These conditions can be boiled down to two: that all effects relevant to the welfare of all individuals be properly priced on the market, and that perfect competition prevail in all economic activities.

Once we depart from this ideal economic setting, however, the set of outputs and prices to which the economy tends may not serve the public so well as some other set of outputs and prices. In addition to this possible misallocation of resources among the goods being produced, it is also possible that certain goods which can be economically justified are not produced at all, while others that cannot be economically justified continue to be produced. If, for example, technical conditions and the size of the market are such that a number of goods can be produced only under conditions of increasing returns to scale (falling average cost), it is possible that, although some of these goods will be produced by monopolies charging prices above marginal cost, other such goods will not be produced since there is no single price at which the monopolist can make any profit. But the production of these latter goods is not necessarily uneconomic. It may simply be the case that the monopolist who sells each good at a single price cannot transfer enough of the benefits from his potential customers to make the venture worthwhile.

Again, certain goods having beneficial, though unpriced, spillover effects also qualify for production on economic grounds; but they cannot be produced at a profit so long as the beneficial spillovers remain unpriced. The reverse is also true and more significant: profitable commercial activities sometimes produce noxious spillover effects to such an extent that, on a more comprehensive pricing criterion, they would be regarded as uneconomic.

2.   The economist engaged in the cost-benefit appraisal of a project is not, in essence then, asking a different sort of question from that

12

being asked by the accountant of a private firm. Rather, the same sort of question is being asked about a wider group of people – who comprise society – and is being asked more searchingly. Instead of asking whether the owners of the enterprise will become better off by the firm's engaging in one activity rather than another, the economist asks whether society as a whole will become better off by undertaking this project rather than not undertaking it, or by undertaking instead any of a number of alternative projects.

Broadly speaking, for the more precise concept of revenue to the private firm, the economist substitutes the less precise yet meaningful concept of *social benefit*. For the costs of the private firm, the economist substitutes the concept of *opportunity cost* – the social value foregone when the resources in question are moved away from alternative economic activities into the specific project. For the profit of the firm, the economist substitutes the concept of *excess social benefit over cost*, or some related concept used in an investment criterion.

3. It cannot be too strongly stressed, however, that even the result of an ideally conducted cost-benefit analysis does not, of itself, constitute a prescription for society. Since it simulates the effects of an ideal price-system, the ideal cost-benefit analysis is also subject to its limitations. Any adopted criterion of a cost-benefit analysis, that is, requires *inter alia* that all benefits exceed costs, and therefore can be vindicated by a social judgment that an economic re-arrangement which *can* make everyone better off is an economic improvement. The reader's attention is drawn to the fact that such a judgment does *not* require that everyone is actually made better off, or even that nobody is actually worse off. The likelihood – which, in practice, is a virtual certainty – that some people, occasionally most people, will be worse off by introducing the investment project in question is tacitly acknowledged. A project that is adjudged feasible by reference to a cost-benefit analysis is, therefore, quite consistent with an economic arrangement that makes the rich richer and the poor poorer. It is also consistent with manifest inequity, for an enterprise that is an attractive proposition by the lights of a cost-benefit calculation may be one that offers opportunities for greater profits and pleasure to one group, in the pursuit of which substantial damages and suffering may be endured by other groups.

In order, then, for a mooted enterprise to be socially approved, it is not enough that the outcome of an ideal cost-benefit analysis is positive. It must also be shown that the resulting distributional changes are not regressive, and no gross inequities are perpetrated.

13

CHAPTER 2

The Pareto Basis of Cost-Benefit Calculations

1. A Pareto improvement is defined as a change in economic organization that makes everyone better off – or, more precisely, that makes one or more members of society better off without making anyone worse off. A *potential* Pareto improvement is, then, defined as a change which – if costless transfers of goods and/or money among members of society are assumed – *can* make everyone better off. It is, in other words, a change which produces gains that exceed in value the accompanying losses; a change, therefore, such that gainers *can* (through costless transfers) fully compensate all the losers and remain themselves better off than before.

It is now asserted that the rationale of existing cost-benefit criteria is ultimately that of a potential Pareto improvement. Ignoring for the present (a) the difficulties of evaluation and (b) the problems that arise when outlays and benefits are expected to appear at different times in the future, the formal requirement of a potential Pareto improvement, and therefore of a cost-benefit criterion, is simple. Let us define a compensating variation, CV, as the sum of money which, if received or paid after the economic change in question, would make the individual no better or worse off than before the change. If, for example, the price of a loaf of bread falls by 10 cents, the CV is the maximum sum a man would pay in order to be allowed to buy bread at this lower price. *Per contra*, if the loaf rises by 10 cents the CV is the minimum sum the man must receive if he is to continue to feel as well off as he was before the rise in price. Since, in general, some people lose and some people gain following any economic change – which may involve a fall or a rise in several product and/or factor prices (or may involve the introduction of a new good or the withdrawal of an old one) – the CVs of the gainers (the largest sums they are able to pay), which is a positive sum, may be added algebraically to the CVs of the losers (the smallest sum they will accept), which is a negative sum. If the resulting algebraic sum is positive, gainers can more than compensate losers, and the change will realize a potential Pareto improvement. If, on the other hand, this algebraic sum is zero or negative, the economic change contemplated does not realize a potential Pareto improvement. Moverover the magnitude of a positive algebraic sum measures the extent of the potential Pareto

14

improvement, while the magnitude of a negative algebraic sum measures the extent of the potential reduction of welfare.

Although it is seldom made explicit, the reader will do well to bear in mind that all calculations that enter into a cost-benefit analysis, when reduced to a single point of time by acceptable methods, are to be interpreted as contributions, positive or negative, to the magnitude of some resulting potential Pareto improvement. What is to be concluded, then, from a cost-benefit analysis showing, say, an excess gain of $100,000 is *not* that everyone concerned *is* made better off in varying degrees; only that it is conceptually possible, by *costless* redistributions, to make everyone better off, in total by an amount equal to $100,000. And since economists have, from time to time, vented their dissatisfaction with the notion of a potential Pareto improvement as a criterion and a measure of social gain, we can hardly employ cost-benefit techniques with a clear conscience without examining some of the criticisms to which the concept has been subjected.

2. First, the potential Pareto improvement test clearly ignores the resulting change in the distribution of incomes. Not only is it true that not everyone is made better off, it is also possible that those in the community who are made worse off are to be found largely among the lower-income groups. A change which makes the rich better off by $250,000 at the expense of the poor, who are made worse off by $150,000, still produces an excess gain of $100,000 for the community as a whole. As such, however, it is not likely to be accepted by all as an unexceptionable economic change—at least, not unless it is to be accompanied by redistributive measures which would make the poor no worse off than before, and possibly better off. A cost-benefit calculation may, indeed, be accompanied by observations on the resulting distribution, and even by recommendations in this respect. But the quantitative outcome of a cost-benefit calculation itself carries no distributional weight, it shows that the total of gains exceeds the total of losses, no more.

Moreover, the appeal of such a test is diminished by its hypothetical nature. A Pareto improvement which positively requires that when some are made better off, no one is actually made worse off, is assured of fairly wide acceptance. It does some good to some, and apparently does no harm to others. A *potential* Pareto improvement, which is consistent with a great many people actually being made worse off, has much less appeal. One factor, however, does make it easier to countenance. The spread over the last century of increasing wealth, and increasing electoral power, has made for egalitarian tendencies.

The more progressive the tax structure, and the more intensive the competition, the more likely it is that a potential Pareto improvement will result in an actual Pareto improvement, or something close to it. In the limiting case of a system of taxes and subsidies designed to maintain complete equality of incomes, every potential Pareto improvement (allowing for sufficient divisibilities) is transformed into an actual Pareto improvement. By redistributive transfers, that is, everybody in fact becomes better off.

In the existing world, however, where projects can have distributionally regressive effects, the economist can, as indicated above, say something about the distribution resulting from the introduction of an otherwise feasible project. If the economist has reason to believe that it will be unambiguously regressive, his duty is to mention it. It may, in some cases, be practicable to combine the project with a distributional scheme. More often than not, the distributional effects on society as a whole are not large. Provided no spillover effects are involved, the *direct* local effects of a number of familiar sorts of project are apt to be progressive. One thinks in this connection of flood-control, electricity generation, irrigation, and the like. Once spillover effects enter the picture, however, the net impact on the local inhabitants can be distinctly regressive. The spillover effects of through-traffic highways, and flyovers, constructed through working-class neighbourhoods, provide a familiar example.

3. Secondly, as a result of the connection between relative prices and the distribution of the collection of goods, it is possible that a movement from one collection of goods, Q_1 to another Q_2, which realizes a potential Pareto improvement, is compatible with the reverse movement, one from Q_2 to Q_1, *also* realizing a potential Pareto improvement.

This apparent paradox is obviously a disconcerting theoretical possibility. It has to be taken seriously in attempts to prove some general propositions, for instance that some international trade is better for a country than no international trade. The possibility of such a reversal actually occurring in the real world, where there are a large number of goods and people, is much smaller, however, than the impression conveyed by a two-good two-person diagram. Moreover, no matter how likely we rate the possibility, it diminishes as the focus of our analysis narrows, and the effects both of distributional changes on relative product prices and compositional changes on relative factor prices, become smaller. Nearly all cost-benefit calculations can be regarded as exercises in very partial analysis. Thus, all prices, outside those pertaining to the project, may reasonably be assumed constant.

4.   At the beginning of this chapter I 'asserted that the rationale of existing cost-benefit criteria is ultimately that of a potential Pareto improvement'. Let me reassure the reader that the assertion is not arbitrary. If he follows the exposition in this chapter carefully, he will perceive that any criterion requiring that social benefits exceed in value all costs incurred necessarily implies the fulfilment of a potential Pareto improvement. And he may accept it that this criterion has to hold both in the large and the small – for a large change of the sort involved in the introduction of some public project, and also for a marginal change in determining the 'optimal' amount of a product or service produced by the project in question. The extension of the criterion to marginal changes should make it apparent that the interpretation of the potential Pareto criterion – requiring that the economic change under review is to be such as to enable everyone to be made better off – is that which also guides allocative efficiency in general. A person who agrees to apply the principles of allocative efficiency needs no new assumption to extend his agreement to the application of existing cost-benefit analysis. In sum both the principles of economic efficiency and those of cost-benefit analysis derive their inspiration from the potential Pareto criterion, and a person cannot with consistency accept the one and deny the other.

Although in the remainder of this volume we shall continue to use the algebraic sum of the CVs as a measure of potential Pareto improvement, it is also possible to use the algebraic sum of the *Equivalent Variations* (EVs). The EV is defined as the sum a person will agree to in order to go without the thing in question. If this thing is a good, the EV is the minimum sum he would accept to go without it. If, instead, it is a 'bad', it is the most he would pay to go without it. For a project in which the gains exceed the losses, the algebraic sum of EVs is negative since the (potential) receipt of a sum carries a negative sign.

Unless the welfare change arising from a project is considerable, each person's CV is about the same magnitude (absolutely) as his EV; that is, what he would pay for a good (or in order to avoid a 'bad') is about equal to the sum he would accept to go without it. But there can be cases where the difference between a person's CV and EV is significant. Prudence then would suggest that both the CV and the EV criterion be used.[1]

---

[1]   A more detailed discussion of this question can be found in Mishan (1975, chs 20, 21 and 60).

CHAPTER 3

Consistency in Evaluation

1. Granted that a cost-benefit analysis seeks to establish the presumption of a potential Pareto improvement, measured in principle as the algebraic sum of all CVs, one must pass from the general concept to specific ways of estimating benefits and costs. The transition can be made by following the convention of the market economy, which regards people both as producers and consumers of goods. If *qua* producers, men are no worse off in consequence of some contemplated economic change but are better off *qua* consumers then, on the whole, they are better off, and a Pareto improvement is achieved. If they are all no worse off *qua* consumers, but better off *qua* producers, a Pareto improvement is also achieved. Similarly, if men are better off *qua* consumers and producers, there is a Pareto improvement.[1] Moreover, the value of goods and 'bads' to men, either as consumers or producers (factor-owners) are not worked out from scratch. Market prices can be deemed to provide these values in the first instance, following which they can be corrected for 'market failure'.

Except for marginal changes – when cost-benefit analysis is of little value – the notion of a surplus, or economic rent, is applicable. For measurement purposes this is customarily divided into consumers' surplus for changes in product opportunities, and rents for changes in factor opportunities. A common practice, however, is to accept factor costs as given but to substitute some measure of consumers' surplus rather than use product prices, or changes in product prices, alone. This asymmetrical treatment is not wholly unwarranted in an economy where factor groupings are few, but where product groupings are many. A project that increases the output of a product or service may result in a large change in its price without appreciable effects on the relevant factor prices. The larger the change in that price, the more important it is to measure the gain, or loss, by consumers' surplus. Nonetheless, while there is some justification for paying more attention to consumer gains and

---

[1] A person is no worse off *qua* consumer if product prices do not rise against him, and better off if, on the whole, they fall. A person is no worse off, or better off, *qua* producer, if, respectively, factor prices do not fall or, on the whole, rise in his favour.

losses than to the gains and losses of factor-owners, we have occasionally emphasized the importance of valuing factors at their opportunity costs in situations where they may differ markedly from their market prices.

2. There may be occasions, however, when the absence of data prevents the economists from putting a value on certain effects resulting from the project. Very often such effects are spillovers, which do not register on the market mechanism. Ignoring envy and other inadmissible external effects, such spillovers can in principle be brought 'into relationship with the measuring rod of money', as Pigou (1932) put it, the correct concept, as indicated, being the CV of each person affected. But although the spillover can be measured 'in principle' there are likely to be difficulties 'in practice' of putting reliable figures on them. What can be done in the circumstances is discussed in the section on External Effects. When nothing can apparently be done, the effects may be described in some detail, and entered into the final table of costs and benefits. There is a temptation to go further than this, however, and leave a space opposite such unmeasurable effects for the so-called decision-maker to fill in.

Recourse to this practice is unsatisfactory. A cost-benefit analysis is raised on a single criterion, that of a potential Pareto improvement, and this criterion is deemed to be related to a provision of some virtual constitution. Even if a political decision were made, say, to build a dam, a cost-benefit analysis of the dam revealing a net loss would be properly regarded as a valid criticism of the political decision – and the decision could be defended only by invoking *other* considerations, for example, equity or national defence. The determination of the value of a project, or of any part or effect of that project, by the political process is either (economically) arbitrary, or else, if it arises from any other consistent body of principles, is in conflict with the allocative criterion from which a cost-benefit calculation proceeds. To add figures derived on one principle to figures derived from some other principle produces a sum that carries no coherent interpretation.

The economist, as well as the political decision-making body, should be aware of this. If the decision of the latter is to place the evaluation of the project in the hands of the economist, the economist must perforce base his calculations on a purely economic criterion. Returning some parts of it to be evaluated by the political process – which in the first instance agreed to be guided by the purely economic evaluation – is to effect a deception and sacrifices meaning on the

19

altar of quantification, in order to save face. If the unmeasurable effect is completely beyond his range of reasonable guesses, so that a decision cannot be reached by the economist on the basis of the measurable data and by reasonable guesswork, he serves the public better by confessing the truth: that, with the existing techniques and information, he is unable to discharge his task.

As indicated earlier, however, although the economist is unable to place a valuation on some critical magnitude, he should provide the public with any information about it that he has (including informed guesses on any aspect of it). Indeed, he should let the public know exactly the sort of question he is trying to answer. What the economist must *not* do in these circumstances is to equate the eventual *political* outcome with the outcome of a cost-benefit analysis. As with any sort of (part) political decision he reserves a right of independent professional criticism.

CHAPTER 4

The Question of Equity

1. The position taken in this book, that the rationale of a cost-benefit criterion derives solely from the concept of a potential Pareto improvement, may seem somewhat restrictive. Amongst other things, it appears to ignore considerations of 'social merit' – other than those which would in any case emerge from the acceptance of a potential Pareto improvement. To some extent, however, this apparent omission can be traced to the existing difficulties of evaluation. If such 'good' things as better health, improved education, expanded recreational facilities, etc., could be satisfactorily measured, the impact of an investment project on these things would indeed be incorporated into the cost-benefit calculation. Other social goods such as better community relations, or a more discriminating appreciation of music or art, might notionally be brought into the calculus, but they are likely to elude attempts to translate them into money values.

On the other hand, the law might well forbid the undertaking of certain enterprises that could realize a potential Pareto improvement, or even an actual Pareto improvement. Thus gladiatorial contests, public exhibitions of obscenity, the sale of hallucinatory drugs, might be forbidden by laws expressive of public opinion even though every person directly affected would freely choose to participate. The reverse is no less likely: the law may enact measures that do not realize a potential Pareto improvement. Issues over which feelings run high, and about which there is no financial complexity, can be more satisfactorily resolved by conventional voting procedures than by cost-benefit analyses. In addition, such political decisions can enact a legal framework that circumscribes the operations of economic criteria—if only to the extent of determining which of the two opposing groups in any conflict of interest has the legal obligation of compensating the other.

2. Turning to these social goods or 'merit goods' referred to above, such as better community relations, more civic participation or the alleviation of poverty, they may be roughly and to some extent arbitrarily measured by what has come to be known as social indicators. The complex of units employed for this purpose will vary

21

from one social indicator to another. Health, for instance, could include longevity, infant mortality, proportional reduction in a number of diseases, the sale of medical goods and services and so on, while the measurement of poverty might include such indices as the proportion of the population living below some chosen real income, or living on what is deemed to be an inadequate diet, or in 'substandard' housing.

Granted the difficulties of evaluation, wherever investment projects are expected to have perceptible effects on social goods that may be measured by such indicators, a number of physical measures can be used as an index of benefit, either alone or supplementary to the evaluated benefits, to be set against the costs of the project.

These social indicators are only just being formulated and are not discussed in this volume. Despite any contributions they will make in the future to our knowledge of the nation's welfare, however, they will not of themselves entail any alteration of the principles of cost-benefit analysis as treated in this volume.

3.   More attention of late has been directed to the questions of equity and distribution. In particular, the impact of large investment projects on the distribution of welfare has attracted the attention of economists.

One form of response to this concern has been an attempt to incorporate distributional effects into a cost-benefit calculation by effectively expressing gains and losses in terms of utility rather than in terms of money. For each dollar of gain or loss to a specified income group there corresponds a particular marginal utility: the higher the income group the lower the marginal utility of a dollar gain or loss. Having transformed all CVs into utility terms, the cost-benefit criterion is met when the gains in terms of total utility exceed the losses. Clearly a cost-benefit criterion that is not met in money terms may be met when translated into utility terms, and vice versa.

The particular weighting systems that have been proposed are of necessity somewhat arbitrary and all assume diminishing marginal utility of income. One method is that of positing a particular form of the utility-income relation. If, for example, one adopts a function that results in a constant elasticity of *minus* 2 with respect to income, a 1 per cent increase in income is to be associated with a fall of 2 per cent in the level of the utility indicator. Alternatively the weighting system can be made dependent upon political decisions taken in the recent past. One way of doing this, proposed by Weisbrod (1968), rests on the assumption that all public projects that were adopted, notwithstanding their failure to meet cost-benefit criteria, were adopted as a result of an implicit set of utility weights attaching to different groups. By comparing a number of such projects these utility weights can be made explicit and, perhaps, become incorporated into the economist's cost-benefit criterion. Another method of weighting, that of calculating a set of weights from the marginal rates of income tax, derives from the premise that the object of a progressive income tax is to share the 'real' burden of the tax equally among all income groups. Thus, if on the marginal dollar of income, the 'rich' (say those in the $100,000 – $500,000 bracket) pay 80 cents, and the 'not so rich' (say those in the $10,000 – $15,000 bracket) pay 10 cents, it will be inferred that 80 cents for the rich has a utility equal to 10 cents for the not-so-rich—or that an additional dollar to the rich is worth only $\frac{1}{8}$ as much as an additional dollar to the not-so-rich.

There can, however, be a number of objections to any method of incorporating differential utility weights into a cost-benefit analysis. First, there is the obvious difficulty of securing widespread acceptance of a given set of weights. Secondly, the proposed utility-weighted criteria are at variance with the allocative principles by which the competitive economy is vindicated. It is sometimes argued that the usual cost-benefit or investment criteria carry an implicit weighting system; namely that one dollar is equal to one util irrespective of who gains or loses, or that one dollar has the same value for both poor and rich. But the rationale of the conventional cost-benefit criteria does not stem from the notion of maximizing or increasing total utility. As indicated, it derives from the notion of a potential Pareto improvement, the value of output being so increased that everyone *can* be made better off by the change in question. Cost-benefit analysis can, then, be regarded as an extension of an efficient price system that would select only those enterprises producing an excess social value over costs. Once cost-benefit criteria depart from the traditional Pareto-based allocative principles, in the manner proposed by these weighting schemes, then clearly public investment projects can be admitted even though the sum of the individual benefits generated by the project falls below the sum of the individual losses incurred—so that, indeed, everyone can be made worse off by its introduction.

Thirdly, no matter how accurate or acceptable are the set of utility-weights proposed, their incorporation into a cost-benefit analysis does not, in fact, serve the purpose for which they are presumably designed—to promote equity, or at least to guard against projects that are distributionally regressive. For whatever the set of weights employed, the resulting utility-weighted cost-benefit criterion could still admit projects that make the rich richer and the poor poorer, especially if the rich persons affected by the project are numerous or are made very much richer.

Although the device of incorporating utility weights into a cost-benefit analysis as a means of enforcing the claims of equity or distribution is evidently unsatisfactory, such claims have to be respected by the economist who offers advice to society. The least he would do is to point up the distributional implications wherever they appear significant. And since he need not affect to be so unworldly as to be in ignorance of society's commitment to greater equality, or to its declared aversion to measures that harden the lot of the poor, the economist can afford, on occasion, to be more emphatic. In particular, wherever an investment project that appears to be advantageous by ordinary cost-benefit criteria causes particular hardship to some groups, the economist should consider the practical possibilities of adequate compensation.

4. Finally, the reader should bear in mind that economic analysis goes beyond the application of cost-benefit criteria. Political decisions to help the less fortunate members of society do not always entail direct cash transfers. The available cash can be used instead to promote economic opportunity among such groups. Financing education or medical services, recreational facilities, the building of dams or irrigation works, the provision of tools, technical equipment and advice, and the establishing of industries or information centres, are all ways in which the state may help others to help themselves. None of these ways might meet a strict cost-benefit criterion. Yet all of them might be regarded as superior to direct cash transfers. The economist can contribute to such decisions to the extent of selecting – within the limits of a number of seemingly equally appropriate ways of helping these groups – those opportunities which yield the maximum social benefit per dollar transferred to such groups. Clearly, the discounted present value of the maximum benefit per dollar invested in these socially approved ways may turn out to be less than a dollar. But such 'investments' have the merit of encouraging people to help themselves.

CHAPTER 5

Measuring Consumers' Surplus

1. The most crucial concept in the measurement of social benefits, in any cost-benefit study, is that of consumers' surplus. For all except marginal changes in the amount of a good, the market price prevailing in a perfectly competitive setting is an inadequate index of the value of the good. Using partial analysis, therefore, the economist engaged in a cost-benefit calculation has to go beyond a simple price *times* quantity measure of the benefits arising from the products or services of a project. Instead, he makes use of the area under the entire *ceteris paribus* demand curve. Even in the fairly common case, when an investment project is designed to save some part of the costs currently incurred in making use of existing facilities – an example would be a bridge built to replace an existing ferry service – the consumers' surplus concept is implicit in the cost-saving calculation. Indeed, the magnitude of this cost-saving is itself no more than a part, the major part it is true, of the horizontal segment of consumers' surplus that is measured by the fall in the price of the service. The remaining segment is the triangular area arising from the additional services demanded at the lower price.

Since the *ceteris paribus* market demand curve explained in textbooks is the required construct, the reader does well to recall what things go into this *ceteris paribus* pound: population of given size and tastes, the prices of all other goods and productive services, and the distribution of society's assets among its members. As we shall see later, a change in any one of these things can alter the shape of the demand curve in question. Any resulting change in the measure of consumers' surplus will then require careful interpretation. For the present, however, the reader should bear in mind that the interpretation of consumers' surplus demands a reversal of the causal direction usually implied in the interpretation of the demand curve. Instead of the eye travelling horizontally, that is, from a given price to the maximum amount consumers are willing to buy at that price, the eye now moves vertically upward: that is, beginning from a given amount of the good offered on the market, the corresponding point on the demand curve indicates the maximum price the consumers are willing to pay for the last unit of that amount.

2. A simple yet workable definition of consumer's surplus (note the apostrophe after the *r*, indicating the surplus of a single consumer) follows that proposed by Alfred Marshall (1925): the maximum sum of money a consumer would be willing to pay for a given amount of the good, less the amount he actually pays. We may extend the idea by thinking about asking a consumer the maximum sum per week he would be willing to pay for only one pint of milk, the maximum sum he will then pay for a second, the maximum for a third, and so on. These sums, which we can speak of as 'marginal valuations', are plotted as the heights of successive columns in Figure II.1. If a price per pint of milk is fixed at, say, twenty cents, he continues to buy additional pints of milk until his marginal valuation is equal to or below the price. Figure II.1 illustrates a case in which the man buys

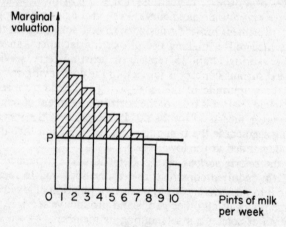

Fig II.1

seven pints of milk at twenty cents, so spending $1.40 per week on milk. The area contained in the shaded parts of the columns above the price line is a sum of money equal to the man's consumer's surplus.

3. Once perfect divisibility is assumed, the stepped outline of the columns gives way to a smooth demand curve. From a point on the vertical, or price axis, the horizontal distance to the curve measures the maximum amount he will buy at that price. The *market* demand curve, being a horizontal summation of all the individual demand curves, can be regarded as the marginal valuation curve for society. For example, the height QR in Figure II.2, corresponding to output

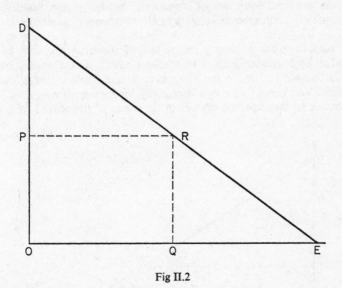

Fig II.2

OQ, gives the maximum value some person in society is willing to pay for the Qth unit of the good – which, for that person, may be the first, second, or n^{th} unit of the good bought. But to each of the total number of units purchased, which total is measured as a distance along the quantity axis, there corresponds some individual's maximum valuation. The whole area under the demand curve, therefore, corresponds to society's maximum valuation for the quantity in question. If, say, OQ is bought, the maximum worth of OQ units to society is given by the trapezoid area $ODRQ$. Now the quantity OQ is bought by the market at price OP. Total expenditure by the buyers is, therefore, represented by the area $OPRQ$ (price OP *times* quantity OQ). Subtracting the maximum worth to buyers ($ODRQ$) from what they have to pay ($OPRQ$) leaves us with a total consumers' surplus equal to triangle DRP.

27

If an entirely new good x is introduced into the economy, and is made available to all and sundry free of charge, the area under the resulting demand curve, ODE (given that prices of all other goods are unaffected) is a good enough measure of the gain to the community in its capacity as consumer. The services provided by a new bridge, or a new park, would be familiar examples. Again, however, if a price, OP, for the service is introduced, the amount OQ will be bought, leaving the triangular area PDR in Figure II.2 as the consumers' surplus. Estimates of consumers' surplus, it need hardly be said, are to be entered as benefits in all cost-benefit calculations.

4. Any investment having the object of reducing the cost of a product or service is deemed to confer a benefit on the community, which benefit is often referred to as a 'cost-difference', or a 'cost-saving'. The benefit of a new motorway, or flyover, is estimated by reference to the expected savings of time, and of the cost of fuel, by

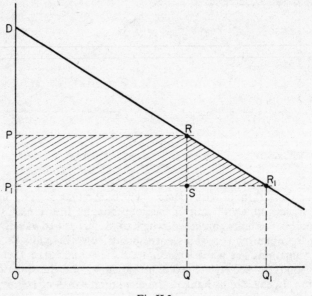

Fig II.3

all motorists who will make use of the new road or flyover. As already indicated, however, the concept of cost-saving is derived directly from the concept of consumers' surplus, as can be shown by reference to Figure II.3. Thus, prior to the introduction of, say, the new flyover in question, the consumers' surplus from using this particular route (being the maximum sum motorists are willing to pay above the amount they currently spend on the journey—an average of OP per journey) is the triangle PDR. If the flyover halves the cost of the journey to them, from OP to OP_1, at which lower cost the number of journeys undertaken is increased from OQ to OQ_1, the consumers' surplus increases from PDR to P_1DR_1, an increase equal to the shaded strip PP_1R_1R. This increment of consumers' surplus can be split up into two parts. There is, first, the cost-saving component, the rectangle PP_1SR, which is calculated as the saving per journey, PP_1, multiplied by the original number of journeys made, OQ. The other component, represented by the triangle SRR_1, is the consumers' surplus made on the additional journeys undertaken, QQ_1, either by the same motorists or by additional motorists. The cost-saving item that enters a cost-benefit calculation is, as indicated, no more than a portion of the increment of consumers' surplus from a fall in the cost of the good. Since it takes no account of the additional goods that will be bought in response to the fall in cost, the cost-saving rectangle alone can be accepted as a *minimum* estimate of the benefit.

We might call this explanation a casual account of the matter, though not a misleading one. Nothing need be said about *utility* since we are not going to translate our money magnitudes into utility terms: the area under the market demand curve, that is, does not become translated into a sum of individual utilities, but remains simply as a sum of their valuations. The extent of the collective improvement from the introduction of a good is, then, expressed in terms of a sum of money which is measured by a triangle of consumers' surplus, such as PDR in Figure II.2. Its interpretation is simply the maximum amount of money the group as a whole would offer in order to be able to buy OQ of this new good at price P. The extent of the collective improvement from a reduction in its price, however, is expressed as an increment of consumers' surplus, as for example the strip PP_1R_1R in Figure II.3. The strip can be interpreted as the maximum amount of money the group as a whole would offer in order to have the price reduced from OP to OP_1.

5. Something more, however, has to be said about this relationship between price and quantity. Beginning from a general equilibruim system, we could deduce that the amount of a good x that is bought depends not only on its own price, but, in general, on the prices of all other goods and factors. In statistical estimates of the price-demand curve for x, the relationship is much more restricted. We

might, for example, try to gather enough data so as to derive a specific equation from the relationship $X = F(P_x, P_y, P_z, M)$, X being the maximum amount of good x demanded, P_x, P_y, P_z, being the prices respectively of the goods x, y, and z, and M being aggregate real income. Goods y and z could be chosen as being close and important substitutes for x, or else y could be a close substitute and z a close complement of x, the relative prices of all other goods being ignored. Sometimes the price of one or more factors are to be included in the function. If, for example, the good x is taken as being farm tractors, the income of the farm population would obviously be a significant variable in the demand for tractors. In any statistical estimate of the price-demand curve for X, the *ceteris paribus* clause will operate to hold constant only those variables, other than P_x, that are included in the function F. All those variables that are not included in the function F – an almost unlimited number of goods and factor prices – are assumed, provisionally at least, to be of negligible importance.

Although this procedure is fairly general, there has been some recent controversy about the M term.[1] If aggregate *real* income is held constant in constructing this *ceteris paribus* demand curve, we are left with a curve which summarizes the pure substitution effect of, say, a declining price. No income-effects are included, and the measure of consumers' surplus derived therefrom will be conceptually accurate.[2] If, on the other hand, aggregate *money* income is held constant, any fall in the price of x raises the real value of an unchanged aggregate money income and – if the income-effect on x is positive – results in some further increases in the amount of x bought (along with changes in the amounts bought of all other goods).[3] The resultant demand curve is a compound of substitution and income effects. In consequence, the measure of consumers' surplus derived from such a demand curve can be no more than an approximation to the ideal measure based on a pure substitution-effect demand curve, as proposed by Friedman (1949). It will be less

[1] A controversy started by Friedman (1949).

[2] Moving along a demand curve for which real income is constant entails an unchanged welfare – no shifting, that is, of the marginal valuation curve because of changes in welfare (or real income).

[3] If a person is willing to pay, say, $5 for the first pint of milk per week and, after paying $5 for the first pint is willing to pay $4 for a second pint, then he would be willing to pay more than $4 for the second pint if he did *not* have to pay as much as $5 for the first pint, but some smaller sum, say $3. For in that case he would be making a consumer's surplus of $2 on the first pint of milk brought, and to the extent that this makes him better off he is willing to pay more (assuming his income-effect with respect to milk is positive) for the second pint.

accurate according to whether the income effect is more important.

However, the difference that arises from using constant *real* income, as against constant *money* income, in the statistical derivation of a demand curve for a single good, is likely to be too slight relative to the usual order of statistical error to make the distinction significant in any cost-benefit study. The emphasis in the *ceteris paribus* pound of the market price-demand curve for x is to be placed, instead, on the constancy of the prices of the goods closely related to x. Thus, the *amounts* bought of all other goods in the economy, including those of y and z, may alter as they please in response, say, to a decline in the price of x. The measure of the consumers' surplus is not thereby affected. Only if alterations take place in the *prices* of the closely related goods, y and z, following a fall, say, in the price of x, does the measure of x's consumers' surplus have to be qualified. For the area under the demand curve for x is a valid measure of the gain to consumers only when the introduction of x, or a decline in its price, is accompanied by access to all other goods at unchanged prices.

CHAPTER 6

Adding and Subtracting Consumers' Surpluses

1. This chapter is a simple exercise in partial economic analysis: the adding and subtracting of consumers' surpluses arising from simultaneous or sequential changes in the prices of two or more goods all (provisionally) having constant costs of production, or constant supply price.

Consider the case where two goods x and y are close, though imperfect, substitutes. In Figures II.4(x) and 4(y) the *ceteris paribus* demand curves for each are the solid lines. D_xE_x is the demand curve for x given that the price of y, p_y, is held constant, and D_yE_y is the demand curve for y given that the price p_{x_1} is held constant. If, now, as a result of some improved method of production, the price of x falls from p_{x_1} to p_{x_2}, the demand curve for y falls from D_yE_y to $D'_yE'_y$ as shown in II.4(y). At the unchanged price p_y, the smaller quantity OB is demanded (rather than OC, which was demanded before the fall in the price of x).

With a lower price of x, consumers are obviously better off. They would, of course, be better off even if they continued to buy exactly the same amounts of x and y as they did before the fall in the price of x. Assume, as a first stage in the argument, that they are constrained to buy the same quantities as before. Then, by removing this constraint, they further improve their welfare by buying more of x, and buying less of y. Having made these changes, and buying now OQ of x and OB of y, how do we interpret consumers' surpluses?

First, the measure of the gain in consumers' surplus is represented wholly by the shaded strip in Figure II.4(x) between the original price p_{x_1} and the new price p_{x_2}. Provided all other goods prices remain unchanged – and, in particular, that of its close substitute y remains unchanged at p_y – this shaded strip measures the most that consumers will pay to have the reduction in the price of x. As for the factors of production that are no longer needed to produce BC of y, they may be supposed to spread themselves among other uses for a negligible change in their prices.[1] This is a long-run assumption that

---

[1] If the demand for x has an elasticity greater than unity, the factor costs of producing OQ units will be greater than those necessary to produce OM units. Some of the factors discharged from y will then move into the production of x. If, however, the elasticity for x is less than unity, factors will move out of x as well as out of y. Provided total consumers' expenditure remains unchanged, factors moving out of x and/or y will find employment elsewhere.

the economist is free to make, but if there are perceptible costs of factor movements they should obviously enter into the calculus.

Secondly, the dotted triangle shown in Figure II.4(y) represents the consumers' surplus in having a price p_y when the price of x is now p_{x_2}. This triangle is the difference between the most they would pay for OB of y (OD'_yRB) and what they have to pay for OB of y (OP_yRB) when x is priced at p_{x_2}.

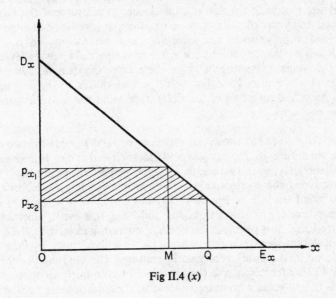

Fig II.4 (x)

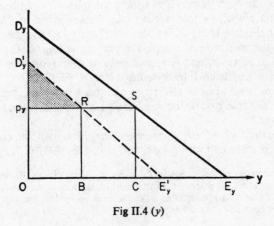

Fig II.4 (y)

Note particularly the interpretation of this reduced triangle of consumers' surplus—that where the demand curve for y shifts inward in response to a fall in the price of x. The reduction of the *initial* area of consumers' surplus, $p_y D_y S$ (corresponding to the original price of x, p_{x_1}) to this smaller area of consumers' surplus $p_y D'_y R$ (corresponding to the lower price of x, p_{x_2}) – a reduction in area equal to $D'_y D_y S R$ – is *not* to be regarded as a loss of consumers' surplus consequent upon the fall in the price of x from p_{x_1} to p_{x_2}. This reduction in area is simply the consequence of consumers' bettering themselves by switching from good y to the new lower-priced good x. Provided supply prices are constant, and we assume they are, the *ceteris paribus* conditions are met, and the partial analysis depicts the consumers' gains ·wholly within the area of the demand curve of the good whose price has fallen—irrespective, that is, of the resulting magnitude and direction of the shifts in demand for all other goods in the economy.

2. Hicks (1956) has shown how the consumers' surplus on two or more substitute goods, say gas and electricity, that are introduced simultaneously, or in succession, can be measured. Suppose that gas is introduced at a given price p_g into an area which has no electricity. The shaded triangle of Figure II.5(g) can be taken as a measure of the resulting consumers' surplus. If, following this event, electricity is introduced at a price p_e, the demand curve for electricity $D_e E_e$ is obviously smaller when gas is available at a fixed price p_g than it would be in the absence of gas. For already the consumers derive much benefit from gas, and the introduction of a fairly close substitute is not so great a boon as it would be if, instead, there had been no gas in the first place. The additional gain to consumers from introducing electricity into a gas-using area is given by the dotted triangle in Figure II.5(e). The sum of these two triangles together measure the consumers' surplus from providing both gas and electricity at prices p_g and p_e respectively. It need hardly be said that if electricity had been introduced at price p_e first, followed by gas priced at p_g, or had both electricity and gas been introduced simultaneously at these prices, the resulting gain to the consumers would be the same.[2]

This method of adding consumers' surpluses can, of course, be extended to three or more goods, and is just as valid if the goods in

[2] Thus, when the demand curves for both gas and electricity are drawn, each on the assumption that the price of the other is fixed, the sum of the areas under the two demand curves can be smaller than the area under the demand curve for either in the absence of the other good.

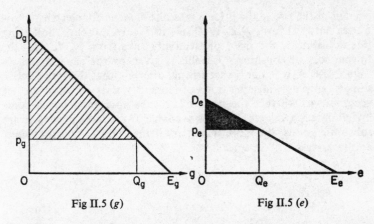

Fig II.5 (g)   Fig II.5 (e)

question are complements rather than substitutes. If, for example, gas and electricity were compliments – as they would be if the only use of electricity were the heating of electric pokers for lighting gas fires—a fall in the price of gas would raise the demand curve for electricity. A subsequent fall in the price of electricity would then provide a larger consumers' surplus than if the price of the complementary good, gas, had not fallen in the first place.

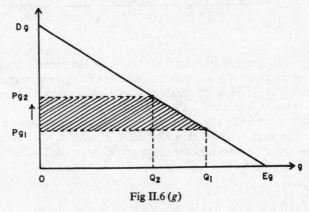

Fig II.6 (g)

3. The further extension of the method to subtractions of consumers' surpluses poses no problem. Suppose once more that electricity and gas are substitutes for one another and that the prices of both rise, as indicated in the Figures II.6(g) and (e).

The loss in consumers' surplus arising from a rise in the price of gas from p_{g_1} to p_{g_2} is shown by the shaded strip in Figure II.6(g). As a result of the rise in the price of gas, the demand for electricity now moves outward from $D_e E_e$ to $D'_e E'_e$ in Figure II.6(e). If, following this adjustment, the price of electricity rises from p_{e_1} to p_{e_2}, the further loss of consumers' surplus is given by the shaded area in Figure II.6(e). It is hardly surprising, after all, that the loss of consumers' surplus when the price of electricity rises becomes greater according to whether the price of its substitute good has become higher or less available. The less available or the more expensive are substitute goods, the more it matters if the good in question rises, and vice versa.

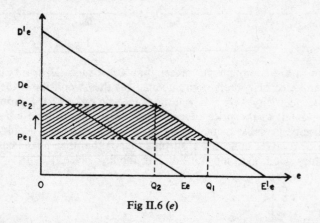

Fig II.6 (e)

If, instead, gas and electricity happen to be complementary goods, a rise in the price of gas causes an inward shift of the demand curve for electricity. The loss of consumers' surplus of any subsequent rise in the price of electricity is then smaller than if the price of gas had not risen in the first place. This also makes good sense since an initial rise in the price of gas makes electricity *less* useful when it is complementary with gas—and not more useful as it will be when it is a substitute for gas.

CHAPTER 7

Measuring Consumers' Surpluses when other things are not Equal

1. When estimating the demand curves for goods provided by new investment projects we have to make allowance over the future for changes in population and changes in real per capita income. Ignoring military considerations, a rise in population without any change in real per capita income is not generally thought of today as conferring an increase in social welfare—unless the state is regarded as having purposes distinct from those of the members of society. Nevertheless, the resulting rise in the demand curves does increase consumers' surplus as defined and, consequently, can make economically feasible particular projects that would, in the absence of population growth, be economically unfeasible.

Population growth and the growth of per capita real income comprise economic growth, and together contribute, over time, to the apparent growth of benefits arising from any investment that is currently undertaken. Clearly the expectations of such growth-induced benefits have to be taken into consideration by the economist who is required to declare in advance the average rate of future growth on which his calculations are to be predicated. Having adopted some acceptable pattern, over time, of aggregate economic growth, he must then determine the way in which the expected economic growth will affect the magnitude of the benefits conferred by the goods that are to be produced by the investment project under examination.

If population alone grows over time (without, that is, any increase in per capita real income) there will be an increase in the demand for the goods produced by an investment project. A bridge or a national park will cater to an increase in the annual number of travellers or visitors over time. As for an increase in per capita income alone (without, that is, any increase in population), an increase in the use made of the bridge or national park is less certain: the average individual's income effect on the demand for the services of the bridge or the national park may or may not be positive. If it is positive, however, although a person pays no more visits to a national park as he becomes richer, his valuation of the same services will be greater than before. This is not because, say, his annual visit to the national park provides him with any more utility than it did when he was less rich, but simply because the maximum sum he is willing to pay for such a visit is higher when his real income, or welfare, is higher. And if, at a constant price level, we make our calculations on the basis of money values, any rise in the value of benefits over time, for all such reasons, must be entered into the calculation.

Where there already exist enterprises similar to that being contemplated, we have to move more carefully. If, for example, the government wants to go in for bridge building when it already has built a bridge A over the river, the building of another bridge, B, is justified simply if the future benefits – as measured by expected consumers' surplus from use of the B bridge – exceeds the capital costs. It would not even matter if the traffic that was expected to use the B bridge, and to generate benefits sufficient to cover its capital costs, had the incidental effect of leaving the A bridge devoid of all traffic. The A bridge has already been built: the capital sunk into it irrecoverable. We need, then, consider only the new costs of building the B bridge, and the new benefits. The demand schedule for the services of the B bridge provides us with a measure of the *additional* benefits to be reaped from an *additional* capital expenditure. The area under this demand curve, that is, provides us with a rough measure of the consumers surplus, which is to be interpreted as the maximum sum that the users of the bridge are willing to pay *when they already have the A bridge at their disposal*.

In the decision to build A, therefore, the magnitude of the annual benefits will not have to be written down after, say, five years, when the B bridge is expected to be opened for traffic. For the benefits (as measured) for the services of the B bridge are additional to those currently anticipated for the A bridge. Again, and for the same reason, in determining the point of time at which the B bridge is to be built, no account is to be taken of the consequent fall in the demand for the services of the A bridge.

2. The increase in consumers' surplus arising from a fall in the price of a good x, all other prices remaining unchanged, is a measure of the increase in society's welfare. If, however, the only change that takes place is a *rise* in the price of a substitute good, y – a change that reduces society's welfare – the demand for x will, as we have seen, shift outward. As a result, the area under the demand curve for x, identified as the consumers' surplus arising from the provision of x, is apparently enlarged. But although consumers as a whole are indeed worse off if the price of y alone is raised, the larger area of

consumers' surplus for the good x does mean that – given all other prices, including the now higher price of y – the gain associated with the *existing* price of x is, in these new circumstances, larger than before. Put otherwise, if y becomes dearer, the loss that would be suffered if the good x were to be withdrawn is that much greater. Consequently, it may well be economically feasible to undertake x-producing investment projects only after the price of y has risen. The economist, examining the future course of the demand curve for x in order to calculate the magnitude of future benefits from its consumption, does *not* therefore need to distinguish between the rises in consumers' surplus for x that indicates an increase in society's welfare and the rises in consumers' surplus that are indicative of a loss in social welfare, the result, say, of price rises or unavailabilities elsewhere in the economy. He accepts as data all the prices and goods over which he has no control, for they fall outside his domain of investigation. If the project is that of investing in an increased output of x, the magnitudes over the future of the consumers' surplus of the increased output of x are to count no matter how they arise.

No exception to this rule occurs if the rise in the price of a good y, or of any other good related to x, is a result of direct government intervention. If the government levies an excise tax on y, or adopts a policy of withdrawing y from the market, the economist is always at liberty to point out the lack of economic justification for such policies, and the consequences that are likely to follow from their implementation. But assuming these policies are to prevail over the relevant time period, he has no choice but to measure the changes in the consumers' surpluses of good x in the usual way.

Only if the economist is engaged in a cost-benefit study that encompasses a number of closely related goods is he in a position to pronounce on actions calculated to change other relevant prices from some generally acceptable pattern, say from that corresponding to marginal social costs. A transport economist, for example, would wish to point out that the apparent increase in the consumers' surplus of private traffic, which seems to warrant investment in road-widening schemes, is the result simply of a reduction in the availability of public transport, a reduction that is itself the result of traffic congestion on existing roads. The imposition of a traffic toll that produces an optimal flow of traffic will increase the efficiency of public transport, and may reduce private motorists' surplus to a magnitude that no longer warrants investment in road-widening. Such a solution is clearly the more efficient one, and that which, in the circumstances, the economist will propose. In contrast, if the economist is required to advise on road widening schemes but is allowed no control whatsoever on the existing volume of private traffic (which may well be greatly in excess of an optimal traffic flow) he has no choice but to accept such political constraints and to calculate the benefits of road-widening under the existing conditions.

3. Changes in the prices of related goods may, however, arise not exogenously, or from government actions, but simply from the fact that their supply curves are not constant but downward or upward sloping. The additional welfare gains and losses that may then be generated from consequent price changes in related goods, following a rise or fall in the price of x, are properly a part of the gains or losses arising from investment in the x project. Though such increments or decrements may not be substantial, provision can be made for including them in the calculation.

Let us illustrate how this can be done by reference to our previous example of the two substitute goods, gas and electricity.

The consumers benefit from introducing electricity at price p_e, when gas is already available at p_g, has been measured as the dotted triangle in Figure II.5(e). Let gas now have an upward-sloping supply curve as shown by SS in Figure II.7. On the introduction of

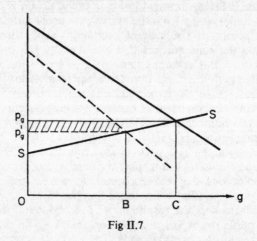

Fig II.7

electricity, the demand curve for gas contracts from the solid line to the broken line, the amount of gas taken being reduced from OC to OB, and the equilibruim supply price falling from p_g to p'_g. The total increments of benefit to the consumers of (i) the introduction of electricity at price p_e, plus (ii) an *induced* fall in the supply price of gas from p_g to p'_g may be calculated by taking them in sequence.

First, the dotted triangle in Figure II.5(*e*) gives (i), the increment of consumers' surplus from introducing electricity at price p_e *with the price of gas at* p_g. Secondly, the shaded area in Figure II.7 gives (ii), the further increment of consumers' surplus for a fall in the price of gas from p_g to p'_g *with the price of electricity remaining at* p_e. The sum of the two areas, then, is a measure of the consumers benefit from (interpreted as the most they are willing to pay for) introducing electricity at price p_e when, as a result, the price of gas to them will fall from p_g to p'_g.[1] An extension of the analysis reveals that if gas has, instead, a downward-sloping supply curve, the leftward shift in its demand curve, following the introduction of electricity, results in a higher price for gas, and therefore entails a further *subtraction* of consumers' surplus.

Symmetrical reasoning applies to goods that are complements. If, for example, gas were complementary with electricity, the introduction of electricity at price p_e causes an outward shift in the demand curve for gas. If the supply price of gas is upward-sloping, its price rises somewhat, and a loss of consumers' surplus in gas has to be deducted from the gain in consumers' surplus arising from the introduction of electricity. If, on the other hand, the supply price of gas were downward sloping, the price of gas would fall somewhat, and to that extent an addition to the consumers' surplus in gas is to be included in the calculation.

To introduce a little more complication, if electricity also has an upward-sloping supply curve, the induced shift in the demand curve for gas and the induced change in the price of gas will itself induce some further shift in the demand curve for electricity and, therefore, induce some alteration in its price as well. A further correction of consumers' surplus is then called for. One can continue in this way indefinitely. But under plausible assumptions (related to familiar stability conditions) these repercussions become smaller and converge to a new equilibrium in gas and electricity.

Since the errors in estimating the relevant demand curves over the future are large enough, it is not usual to bother much about the secondary repercussions discussed above. In the preceding example of the introduction of electricity into a hitherto all-gas economy,

---

[1] If electricity were also an upward-sloping supply curve industry, there would, following the fall in the price of gas, be a further reduction of any initial cut in the cost of electricity. In the newly established equilibrium we should have to take into account this further increment of gain. I leave this as an exercise for the reader, rather than clutter up the text with refinements of this order. For practical problems, economists would be satisfied if the two calculations in the text could be made with tolerable accuracy.

attempts to calculate further additions or subtractions of consumers' surplus according to the shape of the supply curve of gas would be regarded as a refinement. It is unlikely that economists would go beyond a calculation of the primary repercussion.

4.   Consider now a spontaneous shift in the demand from x to y that decreases the consumers' surplus of x and increases that of y, and would appear therefore to warrant reduced investment in x and increased investment in y. Once more the crucial question is whether the economist is asked about investment in y without his having any control or say in the matter of the output and pricing of x, or whether, instead, both x and y come under his surveillance.

To illustrate with a topical example, suppose there is a movement of population over time from London to the Brighton area. Increased investment in social capital, especially in public utilities, will be required in the Brighton area at the same time as existing social capital in London falls into disuse. If we suppose that, prior to the exodus, the amount of social capital was just right in both places, a prospective shortage of 100,000 houses in Brighton would be matched by a prospective vacancy of 100,000 houses in London, There would also be a need to extend schools, build roads, invest more in transport, electricity, gas, water, telephones, and provide additional distributional services in Brighton, all of which would require additional capital, while the equivalent capital investment in London would become superfluous. Clearly, it would have been more economical of society's scarce resources if the desire to move to Brighton had not occurred, for then the existing social capital stock would have sufficed. But, once this change has occurred, the economist is concerned only with ways of meeting it efficiently.

Once social capital is irretrievably sunk in the London area, nothing can be done about it. In the light of existing demands unwanted capital facilities become useless. All that matters now is the economic feasibility of building new social capital in Brighton, where it is wanted. We have, therefore, to compare the additional capital outlays in Brighton with the magnitude of the expected benefits over the future as measured by the demand schedules for the extra services in question.

However, what the migrants into the Brighton area are willing to pay for the services will depend, among other things, on what they are compelled to pay for them in the London area. Only if they had to pay more than the marginal costs of public services in London, could the amounts they would be willing to pay in Brighton be accepted as a correct measure of the benefits there. Indeed, an ideal allocative procedure would require that the managers of these service industries (public utilities, and the like) be ready at all times to reduce the charges for such services to no more than the current marginal costs of providing them, rather than lose a customer. If the economy actually worked in this way, the services of the economist could be dispensed with in such circumstances. But since it is difficult to discriminate between customers in this way, and since extending a reduction in charges made on behalf of one customer to all other customers, involves the company in losses of revenue – such losses being, in effect, transfer payments from the company to its customers – the customary charges are generally maintained.

If this is so, however, it follows that the choice of moving from London to Brighton is being made on the wrong terms. For if, by reducing the charges of one or more of such public services until it is nearer to the marginal cost of its provision, a number of such 'emigrant' families can be induced to stay on in London, then a potential Pareto improvement can be effected: everyone concerned can be made better off as compared with the alternative situation in which such families move to Brighton.[2] The ideal experiment is not to allow any family to move from London to Brighton without first offering it the option of buying all such existing services at their marginal running costs. If, when such terms are offered to potential migrants and they are still willing to move, and to pay for all newly required public services prices which cover their inclusive costs, well and good.

Unless marginal cost pricing is already established in the public utility sector, such an ideal experiment is likely to run into administrative and political objections. For the costs of discovering potential migrants, and of offering them special marginal cost terms without arousing the suspicion and hostility of other households, can be prohibitive.

In the circumstances, since people are constrained to choose whether to stay on or to move to Brighton on the 'wrong' terms, the possible losses are inevitable, and the economist has to regard them as bygones. By accepting a demand curve for electricity based on a *ceteris paribus* clause that includes the prevailing London prices, he concludes that the project is economically feasible if his calculation reveals an excess of benefits over cost – that is, if benefits exceed

[2] If the annual excess over the variable current costs of providing family A with electricity is $100, an effective bribe of $60 would leave the electricity company with $40 more revenue than it would earn if the A family moved. Both the A family and the company are therefore better off than if the A family moved to Brighton.

costs after ignoring losses of quasi-rent arising from the institutional, or political, constraints (which, in this instance, serve to present the potential migrant with the 'wrong' terms).

5. A spontaneous change in taste, from some existing good x to another existing good y, would appear then to involve society in a waste of resources—unavoidable, perhaps, but waste for all that. A part, at least, of the capital invested in the production of x is, for no 'sensible' reason[3] rendered useless, and additional capital has to be built to meet the additional demand for y; additional capital which could otherwise have been used to raise real income. In that sense society is worse off than it would have been had its tastes remained unchanged. This conclusion emerges with greater force if we suppose first, a change from x to y followed, after an interval, by a change in tastes back from y to x again, with the cycle, perhaps, repeating itself. In this way capital is used up which could otherwise – had tastes remained unchanged – have been invested as useful additions to the capital stock.

If, however, under its existing political institutions, society permits the use of scarce resources for the express purpose of inducing these changes in taste – including attempts to shift tastes from x to y, and later from y to x – the social waste can no longer be held to be unavoidable, a consequence only of exogenous factors. Even if the attempts to alter existing tastes are not always successful, one can point to a social loss of those resources that are used up by advertising agencies.[4] Moreover, if we are thinking in terms of a more dynamic economy, and the induced changes of tastes are from x to y, from y to z, from z to w, and so on, where y, z, w, are new sorts of goods which, without persuasion, would not have been wanted (or, at least, not in those quantities), then idle capacity is prematurely brought about in the production of each of these goods, and an unnecessary rate of obsolescence is 'artificially' induced. So long as

[3] Unless economists make judgments about tastes which, up to the present, they have been very wary of doing.

[4] I am concerned only with resources used to persuade people to change their tastes, not with resources used to provide information. I am aware that advertisers have long sought to convince the public that advertising is also entertaining and informative, and even (priced at zero) demanded by the public as a joint product. But there is no great difficulty in maintaining a distinction between the aim of providing partial information (as offered by commercial advertisers) and the aim of providing impartial information (as offered, say, by consumers' associations). Nor is much imagination needed to surmise that if all commercial advertising were to cease, newspapers, and other media, would give more space, and time, to providing information on the goods offered by industry.

the economist remains neutral as between tastes, avoidable waste can be said to be taking place. Such losses, if unexpectedly introduced, are borne by the owners of capital. But once the risk of rapid changes in taste are recognized, they are passed on to the country at large (along with the factor costs of advertising) through the higher prices needed to cover the higher costs of 'artificial' obsolescence.

An investment for the express purpose of changing tastes – as distinct from expenditures necessary to provide impartial information – such as that undertaken by an advertising agency, may be expected to generate a future stream of additional revenues to the producers. The factor costs of the investment in advertising are, of course, paid ultimately by the consumers of the advertised products. But whether this investment creates additional demand for existing or new goods, the additional revenues cannot be interpreted as social benefits. Furthermore, the resulting obsolescence of the plant and machinery, used in the production of these goods from which demand has been removed, can be interpreted as an avoidable social loss. Thus, so long as the economist has no means of ranking tastes, he cannot place any additional social value on the demand for goods generated in this way. The economist's calculations are based on the assumption that existing tastes remain unchanged for the period covered by the calculation. Only on such a condition can he make comparisons between alternative economic organizations.[5]

---

[5] Supposing that the problem of scarcity still exists (a moot point with respect to Western countries), there is a case for society's making provision for using resources in order to avoid spontaneous changes in tastes, and to maintain existing tastes; a better case, I should think, than could be made for the use of scarce resources in order to induce changes in tastes, so effectively reducing the availability stock of capital, or its rate of growth.

CHAPTER 8

Measuring Rents

1. Rent may be defined as the difference between what the factors (or productive services) of a resource owner earn in their current occupation, and the minimum sum he would be willing to accept to keep them there.[1] Like consumer's surplus, it is a measure of welfare change when relevant prices are altered. But whereas consumer's surplus is a measure of welfare gain for a fall in one or more product prices, rent is a measure of welfare gain for a rise in one or more factor prices. Nevertheless, the area above the supply curve of, say, labour does not provide so useful a measure of the labourer's rent as does the area below the demand curve provide a measure of his consumer's surplus. For in the case of a person's demand curve there is a presumption that the welfare effects are small. For a man's current expenditure, at least in the West, is commonly spread over a wide variety of goods each of which – with, perhaps, the exception of housing – absorbs only a small proportion of his total income. Indeed, as living standards rise, the variety of goods offered by the market increases along with the increase in a man's real income. One might surmise, therefore, that the welfare effect will become less important an ingredient in his price-demand curve for any single good.

The case is otherwise for the individual's supply curves, in particular for his supply of productive services, say the supply of labour, skilled or unskilled. If he supplies only one sort of labour to the market, the welfare effect arising from a change in the price of this labour falls entirely on this quantity. It then exerts a preponderant effect. Backward-bending supply curves for individual workers are not regarded as curiosa, a fact which would seem to make the measurement of economic rent rather awkward.

But there is a countervailing feature in connection with individual supply curves, which tends to restore measurability. Notwithstanding the mathematical convenience in postulating an economy in which each individual contributes, in general, to all goods in the economy, spreading his total effort among them – as he spreads his income among all goods – on the equi-marginal principle, this postulate is

---

[1] For more accurate measures of rent see Mishan (1959).

recognized as unrealistic. Nor is it a necessary condition for the model of perfect competition – which model is quite consistent with the more realistic assumption that the worker is constrained in his chosen employment to work a given number of hours, and between stated times. (He may, of course, be offered overtime work, though again it will be subject to constraints on the days and times.) For this reason, there is little point in conceiving of the worker's rent from his employment in precisely analogous terms as his consumer's surplus.

2. In picturing consumer's surplus, we think of the excess marginal valuation over price of the first unit bought, of the second unit bought, of the third, and so on until, with the purchase of the nth unit, the excess is zero. Ignoring welfare effects, the analogous procedure for rent would be the excess of the supply price over the marginal valuations, or minimal sums acceptable to the worker, for each of a number of successive units of labour offered until, again, for some

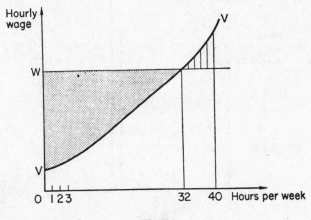

Fig II.8

mth unit of labour offered, the excess became zero. But, as we have indicated in the preceding paragraph, the worker is not permitted to choose his hours of work on the equi-marginal principle. If, on the contrary, he were allowed to, his rising marginal curve VV, in Figure II.8, would intersect the wage-rate line, W, at, say, thirty two hours. His rent would then be the dotted area above VV and below the W line. If, however, the job offered a forty-hour week, and no less,

47

he would be constrained to work eight hours longer than the thirty-two hours that he would choose in the absence of any constraint; and for these eight hours the wage offered is below his successive marginal valuations. On these eight unwanted hours extra he suffers a loss equal to the shaded triangle. His net rent is therefore the dotted area *minus* the shaded area. And, since he is offered the job as an all-or-nothing proposition, he will accept the job only if the difference between these two areas is positive.

Since all workers finding employment in this occupation will be obliged to work the forty-hour week, irrespective of whether they

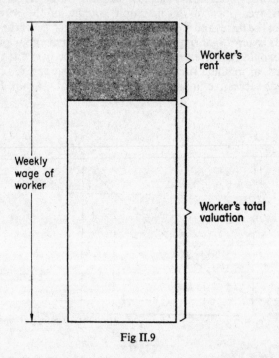

Weekly wage of worker

Worker's rent

Worker's total valuation

Fig II.9

would prefer to work fewer or more hours, the net rent from working the forty-hour week is, for any one of them, the first area less the second area (if any). Letting the worker's weekly (disposable) pay be represented as the area of a unit column with height equal to this weekly wage, as in Figure II.9, the rent is the dotted rectangle measured from the top of the column. By gradually raising the weekly wage and observing the numbers that enter the industry, in response to the higher wage, a supply curve of labour to the industry is generated, and from this we are able to identify the rent of those employed. Thus in Figure II.10, if at the lowest wage, W_1, seven men just agreed to work, they make no rent. If now the wage rises to W_2 and, in response, another ten men are just willing to enter the industry, the first seven enjoy between them a rent equal to the dotted rectangle (W_2-W_1) *times* the distance 0–7. If the wage rises to W_3, and four more men enter, the first seven men between them make a rent equal to (W_3-W_1) *times* the distance 0–7, and the next ten men between them make a rent equal to (W_3-W_2) *times* the distance 7–17, and so we could go on. We are enabled to do this simply because no worker is allowed to alter the number of hours he gives to the industry in response to changes in the wage.

Once large numbers of men are involved the stepped supply curve gives way to a smooth supply curve. The corresponding dotted area

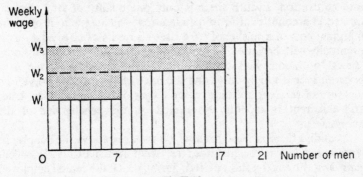

Fig II.10

above this supply curve can then be used as an approximate measure of the aggregate rent enjoyed by those employed in the industry. Its magnitude can be interpreted as the largest sum they would be willing to pay to be in this occupation at the existing wage, given all the other opportunities open to them. An estimation of such rents would always be entered into a cost-benefit analysis of a project if it were known that a wage lower than the existing wage (necessary to attract enough workers to operate the enterprise) would yet suffice to attract *some* workers.[2]

[2] In estimating the rent of the industry's workers by such a supply curve of labour, it is not necessary that labour offered be equally efficient. If, as the industry expanded, the subsequent workers were less efficient than the original ones, costs to the industry would indeed rise. But the measure of workers rent remains unaffected.

3. This area above the industry, or project, supply curve of a factor, which may be used as a measure of the rent of the factors employed there, is to be distinguished, in general, from the area above the supply curve of a firm or industry.

There·are, nonetheless, particular circumstances in which the area above the supply curve for an industry, or firm, can be properly interpreted as a measure of rent. First, there is Ricardian rent in which labour and capital, both of them available in any amounts at constant prices, are applied in fixed proportions to a given quantity of land. The supply curve of the resulting product, say corn, rises, not because of any changes in the supply prices of the variable factors, labour and capital, since, as just stated, their supply prices remain unchanged. The supply curve of corn rises simply because the best land is limited in supply and, as the price of corn rises with an expanding demand, it becomes worthwhile to bring inferior lands into cultivation. Even if there is only one quality of land, though limited in amount relative to demand, rent will accrue to it once the marginal cost of a bushel of corn rises above its average cost—as it eventually will, because of diminishing average returns to additional 'doses' of labour and capital. In these circumstances, the area between such a supply curve and the price of the product provides a measure of the rent accruing to the owner of the fixed factor, land, and this rent is accordingly entered on the benefit side of the analysis.

Secondly, there is the case in which the area above the supply, or cost, curve has to be identified as, what Marshall (1925) called, *quasi-rent*. For over a short period, during which the capital employed by the industry, or firm, is in the specific form of plant or machinery, it is deemed to be fixed in amount, and to have no alternative use. In this short period, then, it partakes of the nature of land, and all its earnings above those necessary to induce it to remain in the occupation (zero in the strict Marshallian quasi-rent concept) are to be regarded as rent. In this short period, then, if the price of the product rises above the per unit variable cost of the product, the resulting excess receipts over the total of these variable costs are quasi-rents; such positive sums making a contribution to the industry's, or firm's, overheads or capital costs.

The above two instances are clear examples of economic rent to a scarce factor. They enter as part of the benefit of producing a given amount of goods during either a short or a long period. Thus, if a given piece of land is used to grow a new crop, or to site some new project, a rise in its rent is part of the benefit of the scheme. If, within a short period, some investment in the industry, or firm, causes its variable costs to fall, the additional quasi-rents that result are to be counted as benefits.

4. The case is quite different, however, when the long run supply curve of a good is produced by two or more factors that are imperfect substitutes and may, indeed, be used in varying proportions. To appreciate the difference with the minimum of effort, let us follow the standard textbook procedure and, first, assume that all firms in the industry are of equal size and efficiency. In that case the rise in the supply price of the good reflects the growing scarcity of the factor that is intensive to the product. With only two factors, say labour and capital, the production of a larger amount of a good x will entail a rise in the price of capital relative to labour, where capital is used more intensively in x than it is in the production of other goods. Owing to the greater weight of capital used in x as compared with its weight, on the average, in other goods, the per unit cost of x rises relative to the unit costs of other goods.[3]

Two things are to be noticed about this rising supply price for the product. First, any point along it indicates the *minimum average cost* for each of the firms in the industry and, therefore, the minimum average cost for that output. Thus, at output Ox_1 in Figure II.11, the minimum average inclusive cost for all firms is given by x_1m_1, and a typical long-period envelope curve for such a firm is represented as S_1S_1. At the larger output Ox_2, the minimum average inclusive cost for the industry is x_2m_2, a typical long-period envelope curve for the firm being represented as S_2S_2.

Second, as the output of the industry expands, the rent of one factor, say that of capital, rises *relative* to that of the other factor, labour—and, unless there are increasing returns to scale, the price of capital will rise in real terms and the price of labour will fall in real terms. Yet neither the shape of the curve, nor the area above it, can be associated with a net gain for both factors taken together. Nor can it be interpreted as a net gain by the producers, or entrepreneurs, each of which makes zero (Knightian) profit[4] in long-period equilibrium.

[3] Put otherwise, if there are more than two goods in the economy, the expenditure on capital, as a per cent of total factor expenditure, is, for x, above the average per cent for the economy as a whole. x's increased proportional expenditure on the higher-priced factor, capital, results therefore in a higher-than-average rise in (relative) cost.

[4] Normal return on capital is not profit, any more than normal return on labour. In the long-period equilibrium, at any point on the industry supply curve, expenditure on factors (both labour and capital) is deemed to be just covered by revenue, leaving no profit, positive or negative, to induce firms to move into, or out of, the industry respectively.

The long-period industry supply curve which, given constant returns to scale, rises only because factor proportions differ as between industries, has to be conceived of as an *average* supply curve for the product. There is no welfare significance attaching to the area above the supply curve.

5. The reader will, perhaps, have noted that no mention has been made of the concept of 'producers' surplus', of which we used to hear a lot until recently. There is no call for it. The concept that is

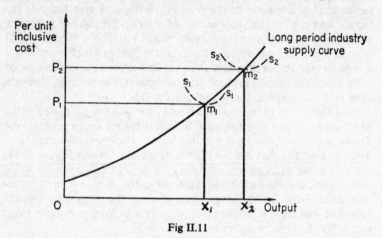

Fig II.11

symmetric with consumers' surplus is that which is known as economic rent, and which we examined in the earlier part of this chapter.

There is, then, no third concept to which a 'producers' surplus' can apply: certainly not the area above the long-period industry supply curve which, as we have just pointed out, carries no welfare significance. True, some instances of economic rent – Ricardian rent and Marshallian quasi-rent – have occasionally been referred to as 'producers' surpluses'. But the use of the term in this connection, or in any connection, has served only to confuse issues,[5] and we shall continue to use only the more generic term economic rent, either (a) *consumers'* rent, or *consumers'* surplus, in so far as the benefits accrue to members of society from a fall in product prices, or else (b) *factor* rents in so far as benefits accrue to members of society from a rise in factor prices.

[5] For a more detailed critique of the notion of producers' surplus the reader is referred to my 1968 paper in *American Economic Review*.

CHAPTER 9

The Economic Cost of Unemployed Factors

1. In general, the cost of factors to the investment project under consideration will be entered as equal to their opportunity costs. The opportunity cost of currently employing a factor in a new project is sometimes stated to be equal to the value it produces in other occupations – more particularly the highest market value it can produce in any enterprise that can make use of it currently. If this definition were accepted, the opportunity cost of bringing unemployed factors into employment would be zero inasmuch as their market value out of employment is zero. Our treatment of rent in the preceding chapter, however, suggests that the opportunity cost of a factor employable in our investment project should be more accurately defined as the minimum sum necessary to induce the resource-owner to place his factors there. Any payment above this minimum sum necessary to attract the factors to this project is, therefore, a rent to the resource-owner, and has therefore to be entered as a component of the social benefit created by the project.

If there is less than full employment in the economy, the project being mooted can have the effect of bringing into employment factors that are involuntarily unemployed, the cost to the economy of using such factors is, in general, smaller than their existing market price. How much less depends upon the period of idleness of such factors expected in the absence of the opportunity provided by the project, and the worth of 'idleness' to the factor-owner. If the unemployed type A labourer, who could be brought into employment by the project, would otherwise remain unemployed for an average period of about a year, then a special price for such A labour used – just enough to compensate the labourer to forgo the 'enjoyment', if any, of his idleness – is to be entered as its cost only for the one year. After that year, it is supposed, this type A labour can be employed elsewhere, and therefore the cost of continuing to use it in this project is equal to its marginal product elsewhere – which, in a competitive economy, is equal to the market price of that type A labour.

Idle land provides another familiar example. If the owner has no personal use for it – neither hunting on it, strolling on it, or getting any pleasure at all from merely gazing at it in its unused state – its opportunity cost to him is nil. If a project can now make use of this piece of land in the production of a good x, and (by discriminating exploitation of its demand curve[1] for x) could offer at most, $10,000 for its use, the whole of this $10,000 would be the measure of additional social benefit from bringing the land into economic use. Whether, after some bargaining by the landlord, the price he is paid is much less, say $2,000, and whether the price is set so that consumers have a surplus of, say, $5,000, the remaining $3,000 going initially to the owners of the business as excess profits, makes no difference to the measure of this additional benefit of $10,000. It affects only the distribution of the $10,000 benefit.

The case is no different if the landowner had entered into a contract with a private corporation, or government agency, giving it full rights over the land for a fixed period. If, after a number of years, the private corporation or government agency, finding no use for the land, is ready to transfer the rights at the rent specified in the contract, or even at a lower rent, the mere fact that the newly negotiated rent (between the government agency, or corporation, and the owners of the new project) enters into the annual expenses of the project activity, does not admit them as costs in the cost-benefit calculation. The opportunity cost of this piece of land to the economy is still nil, and as such it must be entered.[2] Only if an alternative use for this land is discovered, say that of growing potatoes, will its opportunity cost become positive, and equal to the additional value it produces in the potato growing activity.

2.   We may recognize that the land and the landowner are separate entities while, in the case of labour, the services of the labourer and the labourer himself are inseparable. This difference may have important philosophical and social implications. But in economics the distinction is not of itself significant. It may, however, produce a difference of degree. For there is a likelihood that workers attach greater value to the 'idleness' – or, more precisely, to the 'non-market activities' – of their factors than do landowners.

---

[1]   The perfectly discriminating monopolist is, of course, a fictional character who, by discriminating among each of his consumers, and charging each the maximum for successive units, manages to appropriate for himself the whole of the consumers' surplus.

The revenue of the discriminating monopolist can be taken as equal to the consumers' surplus of the quantity he sells, if it were all priced at zero.

[2]   Exactly the same argument applies to any other asset, plant, equipment or piece of property, that contributes nothing, outside its contemplated use, to anybody's satisfaction.

Indeed, the value attached by factor-owners to the non-market activities of their factors can bear yet more emphasis in this connection. The fact that the marginal product of labour in agriculture, in some parts of Asia, is nil does not warrant its being costed at nil in the evaluation of any industrial project. It may be true that labour in the fields may be used until its marginal physical product is nil. It is true, therefore, that if the labour were transferred elsewhere, its apparent opportunity cost *in terms of the physical output or market value it produces in agriculture* is also nil. Indeed, we are to suppose it is nil. But guided by the Pareto principle, which admits only those changes that can make everyone better off, the opportunity cost of employing this labour elsewhere is equal, in this case, to the value the worker himself places on his employment in agriculture. More precisely, and ignoring costs of movement, it is equal to the minimal sum that would induce him to leave agricultural employment and take up employment elsewhere.[3] And this sum can be a small or a large fraction of the going industrial wage in such regions, according to the value the worker places on his leisure, on the stigma (if any) of being unemployed, and on the non-market opportunities open to him. *In the absence* of restrictions imposed by labour unions, and *in the absence* of transfer payments such as unemployment benefits, the cost of drawing labour into industry from an existing pool of unemployment, or a pool of agriculturally 'superfluous' labourers, would appear in a competitive economy simply as the supply price of the additional labour required by industry.[4]

[3] In certain areas of Asia small holdings are large family affairs, and though the marginal product of a person working on a holding is nil, each person (or each family) is paid a share of the proceeds, equal, say, to the average product. If a person is indifferent to all but the pecuniary aspects of the job, he would consider his opportunity cost as equal to his share, or average product. If, then, he were moved elsewhere agricultural product would not diminish, and the remaining members of the farm could afford to pay him the same share without their being any worse off. Anything he could produce elsewhere now adds to aggregate product, and any earnings he receives makes him better off than before. But once we admit that he is not indifferent to non-pecuniary factors, that he prefers to be with the larger family, and that the larger family prefer his presence among them, the value of any additional goods he produces elsewhere must be enough to compensate him and the remaining members, among others, if there is to be a Pareto improvement.

[4] As the reader may know, schemes for moving unemployed labour, or agriculturally 'superfluous' labour, in economically backward countries, into industry have occasionally proposed that such labour be valued at zero; equal, that is, to its marginal product. At the same time, it is also admitted that a positive wage would be necessary to attract such 'idle' labourers from their wonted pursuits. Schemes that would appear feasible by this logic (contrary to that in the text) might not be justified on the Pareto principle.

We have so far ignored the costs of movement, not because they are unimportant but simply because there is little the economist can say about them except that they may well be the greater part of that minimal payment necessary to induce a man (and his family) to move to a new locality. They include not merely the money costs incurred in moving house but the subjective costs – the sense of loss and disruption in parting from old friends, from a known neighbourhood and a familiar pattern of social life. The economist has no choice but to accept the wage-earner's decision to move his family in response to a certain sum as indicative of the (minimum) opportunity cost of his employment in the new project.

3. In times of low employment there is obviously a stronger case to be made for public projects since they act to absorb otherwise idle resources. The additional employment generated is sometimes regarded as a social good to be evaluated and placed on the benefit side. Alternatively, and as an extension of the above treatment, the advantages of public investment in times of low employment are made manifest by reference to the cost aspect. For where there is substantial unemployment, the opportunity cost of labour, skilled and unskilled, and indeed of specific forms of capital equipment, is much lower than if such factors are already employed. Thus investment projects that would not be economically feasible under conditions of full employment may be economically feasible under conditions of low employment—assuming, of course, that employment is expected to remain low, at least in the absence of these investments.

Now if the public investment in question is to generate additional employment, it has to be financed by 'new money'. In other words, in order to create additional excess aggregate demand in the economy there must be no offsetting reduction of aggregate expenditure elsewhere. The additional money required for these investments can be created directly by the banking system: the central bank, for instance, can create the money needed by the government to finance the (additional) budget deficit that arises from government expenditures exceeding their tax revenues. If $1 billion is to be spent on the public projects, then a 'first round' increase of income amounting to $1 billion requires that the $1 billion be raised *without* reducing expenditures elsewhere. Raising a part of this sum through taxation, which reduces current expenditures elsewhere by, say, $\frac{1}{4}$ billion, implies that the initial increase of aggregate incomes will only be $\frac{3}{4}$ billion.

Since, in general, an additional aggregate expenditure of $1 billion will generate multiplier effects that will result in the creation of an addition to aggregate income in excess of $1 billion, cost-benefit calculations that take no account of these secondary income and employment effects will underestimate the net benefits of the projects involved. Although allowance for these secondary income effects should obviously be made – at least wherever, under existing political circumstances, no alternative ways of expanding employment are anticipated – we shall restrict ourselves in the remainder of this chapter to the *primary* employment effects; to costing the hitherto idle resources used by the specific public projects in question.

Though not essential to the argument, we can assume that, prior to the introduction of any one or a number of additional public investment projects, prices in the economy are stable. On this assumption, the effectiveness (in terms of generating additional employment) of the deficit finance associated with the introduction of one or more public investments will depend upon the resulting rise, if any, in factor and product prices. Since this effectiveness in generating employment can be expressed in terms of the probability of drawing the project's factor requirements from the existing unemployment pool, there will, in principle, be a relationship between this probability and the overall rate of unemployment.

This relationship will, of course, depend upon the specific kinds of factors required by the investment project and their location with respect to the project. Primarily, however, this relationship, between the probability of drawing factors from the idle pool and the rate of unemployment, will depend upon the rise in prices (if any) that results from the introduction of this particular project in the given unemployment situation. Much, therefore, depends on the size of the project—or, rather, its factor requirements relative to factors available in the unemployment pool.

4.   To illustrate with extreme examples. Suppose first that overall unemployment is so high that all prices, product and factor, remain constant over the period. Then it may well be that, say, one thousand construction workers required to implement the investment project are initially attracted, not directly from the existing pool of unemployed construction workers, but from existing industries in which they are employed, say industries *A, B, C* . . . But since there is no reduction in total expenditure on the goods produced by industries *A, B, C* . . ., these industries will have to restore the numbers of construction workers in order to maintain their outputs. They can do so only by attracting such workers from other industries or else from unemployed construction workers. Provided that prices remain constant, as assumed, and particularly that the wages of construction

workers remain unchanged, the excess demand for one thousand construction workers cannot be satisfied until they are ultimately drawn (or trained) from the unemployment pool.

If the maintenance of constant prices requires, say, 25 per cent unemployment then we should associate 25 per cent unemployment with factor requirements being met wholly from the unemployment pool. More particularly, if it required 25 per cent unemployment among construction workers within some given region, to ensure constancy of their wages, the economist would associate 25 per cent unemployment among them with an eventual 100 per cent withdrawal of construction workers from the unemployment pool—irrespective of the proportion that might initially be withdrawn elsewhere, say from industries A, B, C . . .

Now suppose, instead, the other extreme – overall unemployment being so low that an additional $1 billion of excess aggregate demand is wholly absorbed in price rises. In particular, let us suppose that the $10 million that is earmarked to pay the wage-bill of 1,000 construction workers has the effect only of raising the total wage-bill of the existing population of 10,000 construction workers by the whole of this $10 million – a rise in their wages, let us say, of 10 per cent; that is, from an initial total wage-bill of $100 million to $110 million. If we now discover that unemployment among construction workers is 4 per cent, then a 4 per cent unemployment rate among them is to be associated with an eventual zero per cent probability of construction workers being drawn from the unemployment pool.[5]

The more usual case follows in an obvious way and can be illustrated by supposing that, with an 8 per cent unemployment rate among construction workers, of the $10 million of initial excess expenditure on construction workers some $6 million is added to the wage-bill of the existing 10,000 construction workers, leaving only $4 million to be spent on hitherto unemployed construction workers. Thus, in the existing employment situation, the attempt to attract 1,000 construction workers into the new project has resulted in only a small proportion of that number being eventually withdrawn from the unemployment pool. The demand-induced rise of factor prices of, say, 8 per cent absorbs $6 million of the sum of $10 million earmarked for construction workers, the remaining $4 million giving employment to only 377 additional construction workers at the new wage of $10,600. As a result, 8 per cent unemployment among construction workers is to be associated with a probability of

[5] Where prices rise in response to the new projects, the real value of sums proposed – here amounting to $1 billion – has to be deflated accordingly.

about 37½ per cent of the required labour being eventually withdrawn from the unemployment pool.

Such a relationship, indicated in Figure II.12, between the probability of drawing a worker of any specified skill from the unemployment pool and the rate of unemployment among that group can be discovered and made use of in evaluating public

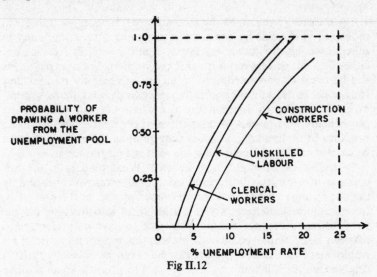

Fig II.12

projects. Thus if the opportunity cost of any particular unemployed skilled worker, say the construction worker, is reckoned to be $4,000 per annum and that of an already employed construction worker – following an induced rise in their earnings to $10,600 – is reckoned to be about $12,000 on the average, then the total opportunity cost to the project of attracting 1,000 construction workers (when unemployment among them is 8 per cent and, therefore, the probability of drawing an unemployed construction worker is about 0.375) is calculated as a weighted average, namely,

$$\$4,000\ (0.375 \times 1,000) + \$12,000\ (0.625 \times 1,000) = \$9\ \text{million}.$$

The opportunity cost of 1,000 construction workers is clearly less than their total wage bill since, in general, it will not be possible to pay the hitherto unemployed construction workers less than those being drawn from existing employment.[6]

[6] For an introduction to an ambitious attempt to construct such relationships for all resources (though without explicit mention of the effects of deficit finance on rising prices) see Haveman and Krutilla (1967).

CHAPTER 10

Transfer Payments

1. A transfer payment, as the term suggests, is simply a transfer in money or kind made by one member or group in the community to others, one which is made *not* as payment for services received but either as a gift or as a result of legal compulsion. Transfer payments can be overt or concealed, and voluntary or compulsory, and they can appear as costs or as benefits to particular persons, firms, groups, or industries. But to the economy as a whole they are neither costs nor benefits; only a part of the pattern of *distributing* the aggregate product. In undertaking a cost-benefit analysis the economist must be careful to exclude them from the relevant magnitudes.

Consider first unemployment benefits. What matters in the calculation of a project that creates additional employment is simply the opportunity cost of the otherwise unemployed workers—that is, the minimum sums necessary to attract them into working for the new project. Where the worker is deemed to have no preference as between being employed or unemployed, the opportunity cost of his employment in the new project can be taken as equal to zero. It follows that if his labour can now be used to produce some positive added value, even if it is no more than $1 worth of output a week, society is, to that extent, better off. In such circumstances his labour, wherever used, enters a cost-benefit calculation priced at an opportunity cost of zero.

As already indicated, however, in the more general case in which the worker does have preferences for one occupation rather than another (even though the preferred occupation pays no more, and possibly less, than the other) the opportunity cost of employing him on the project is *not* his foregone earnings, which, as stated above, will be nil if he is unemployed. If working is, on the whole, regarded as a disutility, the sum required to compensate him for his efforts will be positive, being larger the less enjoyable is the work as compared with being unemployed. If, on the other hand, he positively resents being without employment, this compensatory sum will be negative. This implies that, if necessary, he will pay up to some maximum weekly sum – say $10 a week from his savings – in order simply to be employed in a particular occupation. If so, the opportunity cost of his labour in that occupation is *minus* $10. Though his labour produces zero marginal product, or a negative marginal product that is not so little as minus $10, there is a potential economic improvement in bringing him into employment.

2. Unemployment benefit, whether it is collected by the worker 'as of right' from an insurance scheme, or whether it is wholly or partly government relief, is to be regarded, in a cost-benefit analysis, as a transfer from the earning members of society to the non-earning beneficiary. Nor does it matter whether the money paid to the unemployed worker is from taxes, from loans, or from an issue of new money. For, during the period of his unemployment, the worker does not add to the market value of the aggregate product, this being the result of the contributions of other members of society. Yet he is entitled to, and does consume, a part of that product. It follows that no part of this transfer payment to him should enter as the opportunity cost of his being employed in some industry.

Nevertheless, although this transfer of money to him is not itself the opportunity cost of his labour, the amount of the transfer does affect the level of his welfare and, therefore, also affects the magnitude of the opportunity cost. If, for instance, there were *no* unemployment benefits, he might overcome his dislike of taking on a certain job in exchange for a weekly sum of $8, whereas if his unemployment benefit were $25 a week, it might require a weekly sum of $40 at least – an excess of $15 above his unemployment benefit – to induce him to accept the work. In the former case, the opportunity cost of his labour is $8. In the latter case it is $15 – the *excess* above his unemployment benefit he would require to agree to do the job. If, therefore, his marginal product in this employment were above $15, say $17, he should be given the job. For the worker, when paid $40, will be as well off as before, and the remainder of society will be better off by $2. (The rest of society gains the $25 it no longer has to transfer to the worker, and in exchange gives up only $23 as a subsidy needed to make up the difference between his marginal product ($17), and his wage ($40).)

If, on the other hand, being employed of itself had a positive utility for the worker, an excess of earnings above unemployment benefit would be unnecessary. Indeed, he would be willing to take the job for as little as, say, $20; that is, to give up $5 a week in order to have the job. In that case, the opportunity cost to the industry which employs him is *minus* $5. If his marginal product in that industry is, as before, $17, the social gain is $22.

In sum, accepting the initial distribution of welfare as determined by the *status quo*, which also involves an acceptance of the existing rates of unemployment benefits, the compensation required by an unemployed worker to move him to a particular occupation – measured as the minimum wage he will accept for that job *less* the transfer of unemployment benefit – has to be regarded as the opportunity cost of his labour to that industry. In order to realize a potential Pareto improvement it is necessary only that the social value of his product in that industry exceed this opportunity cost.

Finally, unemployment benefit that runs for a limited period, or falls away gradually, or precipitately, after a certain length of time, introduces only an obvious qualification. If, for example, unemployment benefit runs for exactly six months, a man is likely to accept a lower wage after the elapse of five months than after the elapse of only five days. This eventuality, however, poses no conceptual problem. Economists have to accept the decision of any factor-owner concerning the minimum worth of his factors, and therefore his compensating variation, in whatever circumstances the factor-owner finds himself.[1]

3. The obverse of the benefits or direct subsidies received by unemployed persons are the direct taxes paid by employed persons and private firms. Although private firms properly assess the profits of their enterprises net of all the taxes they pay, the economist interested in *social* cost-benefit analysis – which is tacitly understood by the term cost-benefit analysis, unless prefixed by the word *private* – values all benefits gross of tax. If, out of a $100,000 per annum benefit resulting from the construction of a dam, $35,000 is paid from the gross revenues as direct taxes to the government, this transfer of $35,000 to other nationals, via the central government, does not of itself entail a loss for society. If a number of people benefit from the dam to the tune of $100,000, after all costs are incurred, the fact that between them they transfer $35,000 to other

[1] In the case of capital, however, occupational preferences can be disregarded, leaving opportunity costs to be determined by earning differentials alone. If, in a short period, existing machines are specific to their existing function, their value elsewhere is nil and, therefore, their opportunity costs are nil. If, on the other hand, the machines have a range of uses (as, for instance, lathes) they can, at some cost of conversion, produce a value in other uses. In that case opportunity costs are positive. In any cost-benefit calculation, an existing machine has to be valued at this opportunity cost. Where such a machine has an existing number of alternative uses, it is clearly to be valued at the highest of the alternative opportunity costs. Earnings above this *highest* opportunity cost (sometimes known as its transfer price) are defined as quasi-rents, and accrue to the owners of the machine. In a cost-benefit analysis, however, we need consider only the benefits in excess of these, and other, opportunity costs.

members of society entails a spreading or redistribution of the benefit of $100,000, but not a reduction of it.

In contrast, however, the acceptance of the conventional nationalistic scope of cost-benefit analysis requires not only that estimates of consumers' surplus be excluded, since this surplus accrues to foreign and not to domestic consumers. The benefits to the home country must also exclude all taxes levied on the gross proceeds that are levied by foreign governments. Moreover, these gross proceeds of a particular foreign investment can be reckoned as gross revenues to the home country *only* if that investment has no effect on the sales of goods produced by plant and equipment established abroad by previous investment from the home country. If, for example, a new investment in the foreign country B, by the nationals of the home country A, produces goods which are substitutes for those already being produced in B from previous investments made there by country A, any loss of profits sustained on these previous investments have to enter as part of the costs of the new investment.[2]

If, on the other hand, the new goods are complementary to those produced by plant and machinery already invested in country B by the nationals of country A, the additional profits earned by these older investments have to be added to the expected gross revenues of the new investment.

4. So far we have followed the convention of restricting the jurisdiction of a cost-benefit analysis to the citizens of the nation state. Within the nation's territory, that is, all transfer payments are disregarded in evaluating public investment projects. As indicated above, however, such transfers are not to be disregarded if they take place across national territories. A tariff on foreign imports may be held to benefit the tariff-imposing nation even though it inflicts a loss on foreigners that exceeds the gains of the tariff-imposing nation.

Although this convention is plain enough as between nations, problems can arise when political decisions taken within a country appear to impose jurisdictional constraints.

To illustrate, the central government may have agreed to give a bounty to any local authority undertaking to build a hospital, or a road, to certain specifications. In the absence of the bounty, we can

---

[2] In the limiting case of a continuous demand curve in country B for a good *x* produced there as a result of previous investment goods from country A, the same investor in country A reckons his revenues not by reference to the price of *x* but by reference to *x*'s *marginal revenue*. In such a case, the economist follows suit.

suppose, none of the projects would be admitted as economically feasible, whereas each of them would be if the bounty were entered into the calculation as a net benefit, or as a contribution to the costs—as undoubtedly it would be by the local authority.

It may, of course, be argued that the bounty offered by the central government is, at least, equal to the net benefits enjoyed by the rest of the nation – which includes all those people other than the local citizens having direct access to the hospital, or road, and whose expected benefits have been entered into the calculation. But since the cost-benefit calculation should, in any case, take account of the benefits to be experienced by everyone in the nation, there is no economic justification for separately including the amount of the bounty on the benefit side. On a strict interpretation of the Pareto principle there is no warrant, then, for admitting a project that would, in the absence of the bounty, be regarded as economically unfeasible.

The bounty, it may then be alleged, is granted in consideration of some benefit to the nation at large that is difficult to quantify. A broader, or longer, highway than would otherwise be undertaken, or a hospital having underground facilities, may have a military value for the nation which the economist, or any one for the matter, will find difficulty in appraising. The economist may be able to salve his professional conscience by entering the value of the bounty as equal to the additional security provided for the nation by the project – leaving it open to experts, however, to argue that the same additional amount of security could be provided at smaller cost.

If, on the other hand, no such considerations are present, the bounty is no more than a transfer from the nation's taxpayers to the present and future inhabitants within the locality – notwithstanding which, government authorities may insist that the bounty be entered as a cost-saving item in evaluating the project. In such cases, the economist, as a practical matter at least, may have to comply; his calculations are, in effect, being subjected to political constraints. For all that, he should make it quite clear in his report that the calculation is subject to this political element and that, on a strictly economic calculation, the bounty cannot be treated as a benefit, or cost-saving, item.

This is not the first occasion in this volume, nor will it be the last, that political, or institutional, constraints will have to be considered. Wherever such constraints affect the outcome of the evaluation, in particular where, in their absence, the investment decision would be otherwise, the economist has the duty of making the fact abundantly clear. Not even majority opinion is to be treated by him as the considered opinion of the nation, the voice of the people in council.

Political decisions may be poor decisions for a large number of reasons too tedious to recount.

Finally, the reader may be reminded that the economic criterion employed by the economist is one that is independent of voting procedures and, therefore, independent of the outcome of any particular political debate. In the last resort, the further information and analysis the economist can offer become a part of the contribution to a more informed debate which may occasionally reverse preceding political decisions.

CHAPTER 11

Double Counting

1. The error discussed in the preceding chapter is that of counting transfer payments as costs or benefits. Another error is that of counting real costs or real benefits not once but twice, or more than twice.

Consider the rise in land values that results from economic growth or from population movements, either those arising spontaneously or those following the construction of a railway or road between two towns.

It is sometimes alleged that a rise in rents paid by restaurants, shops, gasoline stations, etc., in some new locality, or along some new route – which rents reflect the increased benefit derived from such facilities by migrating families, or by additional drivers or passengers – may be ignored inasmuch as rents elsewhere will have fallen. There is, it is argued, simply a shift in rents, a result of a shift in demand from one area to another, or from one route to another.

In the absence of economic growth, this can be true. But where it is true, it is a reflection of the belief that the *flow* of additional benefits in some areas is equal to the *flow* of additional losses in other areas. If economic growth is supposed, the flow of some additional benefits will exceed the corresponding flow of losses. What one has to guard against, is counting the same benefit or loss twice; once as a flow, and again, later, as a change in asset-valuation derived from the flow.

The annual rent of a particular site is, in the first instance, a transfer to the landowner of the annual excess profits made by the owner of the business established on it. And these excess profits are, themselves, nothing more than a transfer to the owner of consumers' benefits from the services that are sold on the site. Provided, that in the case of people who transfer their custom to this business, the transfer was made on the proper terms (the services of the business from which they transferred their custom being offered at their marginal cost) any excess valuation above costs of these additional services furnished by this business should, in any case, be entered into the relevant cost-benefit calculation. If this site were to be sold, its market price would be the capitalized value of the now higher expected stream of rents. However, the rise in the stream of rents to this particular site – the result of the excess profit, arising from the increased demand (and increased consumer valuation) of such services – has been, or should have been, entered into the calculation of the flow of benefits. Since in any case such benefit streams are to be discounted to the present in a cost benefit calculation, in order to compare them with capital costs, we must not, in addition, include increased site valuations.

To illustrate, if the construction of a railroad from A to B raises the market value of those houses that are situated near the new railroad station in A, these capital gains are not to be brought separately into the calculation of benefits. The value of such houses rises simply because, once the railroad is built, their occupants have additional advantages either for job opportunities, shopping opportunities, or outings. The estimate of these advantages already have, or should have, been entered into the cost-benefit analysis of the railroad on an annual basis. Therefore to add their capital gains as well would amount to a clear case of double-counting. Needless to say, the same remarks apply to the capitalized stream of the value of any disadvantages that arise from the siting of the stations, or from the construction of the railroad.

2. Again, if this new railroad so reduces the time and increases the convenience of travel as to offer new job opportunities to a number of men, we ought *not* to include the measure of these new rents (a measure of the increase in their welfare from switching to the new jobs) as *additional* benefits. For such benefits are already subsumed in the (potential) consumers' surplus of the new railroad. Such a measure of consumers' surplus – approximated, say, by an estimate of the potential demand schedule for train journeys per annum – reveals the maximum sum each person will pay for a number of train journeys. And in determining this maximum sum, he will take into account the rents of the new job and, indeed, all other incidental utilities and disutilities accruing to him from the new railroad service.

The same *caveat* also applies where the consumers' surplus measure of benefit, that arises from reducing the cost of a good, comprehends the additional profits enjoyed by a number of intermediate agents that handle the good.

Consider, for example, an irrigation project that reduces the cost of grain production over an area. The benefit, to be placed against the costs of the project, is to be reckoned as the saving in costs of production on the existing output *plus* the area of the triangle of surplus (representing the excess of value over cost of the additional output demanded at a lower price that is equal to the new and lower cost). Once more, however, any rise in the profits of farmers, or of grain merchants, or of bankers, and so on, is *not* to be entered as benefits additional to this full cost-saving of the irrigation project. Such items are to be seen as transfers of part of this benefit from consumers to farmers and middle-men—at least during some period of adjustment in a competitive economy. Put more generally, the calculated benefit arising from the lower resource cost of grain is distributed among consumers, farmers, and middlemen, according to market forces and institutions.[1]

---

[1] It may be thought that additional sales, or processing, of grain should raise the profits of middlemen and millers since, at an unchanged mark-up, they handle a larger volume of grain. Yet inasmuch as it requires some additional services to handle an additional volume of grain, the rise in profits is to some extent a private rather than a social gain, for existing workers may have to work harder without a commensurate rise in earnings. To the extent this is not so, there can be short-period quasi-rents which disappear in the long period when additional factors are brought into grain distribution and processing so as to restore normal profits there.

CHAPTER 12

Shadow Prices

1. There is nothing very special about the notion of a shadow price. In evaluating any project, the economist may effectively 'correct' a number of market prices and, also, may attribute prices to unpriced gains and losses that it is expected to generate. If for each hour spent at tennis, a person saves about $1 on medical expenditures, the shadow price of an hour's tennis would be the market price *plus* (at least) $1. Wherever the amounts of a good, to be added to or subtracted from the existing consumption, are large enough, the economist will substitute for price the more discriminating measure of benefit, consumers' surplus. Certain gains, or losses, to an enterprise he will value as zero, since for the economy at large they are only transfer payments. The cost of labour that would otherwise remain idle, he must value at its opportunity cost, not at its wage, and so on.

Nonetheless, the term has been used more specifically in a number of connections[1] and it will, perhaps, avoid confusion if these are briefly indicated.

First, the term is commonly used in mathematical programming problems as an appropriate interpretation of the 'dual' solution to the value of the variables. Such shadow prices are no more than the correct input prices that are consistent with a maximum value of the combination of outputs with the enterprise earning zero profits. We shall not, however, be using the term shadow price in this specialized sense.

Secondly, the term shadow price has been extended to cover the worth of social benefits or losses that are either unpriced by the market or else unsatisfactorily priced. Unpriced or unsatisfactorily priced benefits or losses may be valued by adopting the price of similar things in other parts of the country, or by calculating the spillover effects either by reference to market prices or by other methods. With respect to the former method of pricing, no generalization can be made about it that is at once useful and not obvious, and we shall therefore say no more about it here. Correcting the market prices for spillover effects, on the other hand, is a specialized subject in itself and the treatment of it is consigned to Part III.

[1] The interested reader is referred to Roland McKean's excellent article, 'The Use of Shadow Prices' (1968).

Thirdly, and though clearly related to instances of unsatisfactory pricing by reference to the market, the term shadow pricing is associated with economic calculation in countries – often poor countries – in which prices do not properly reflect relative scarcity, whether of finished goods or of materials, and whether these are produced at home or imported. The inadequacy of prices (as indicators of relative scarcity) arises from a number of factors that interfere with the working of markets, both domestic and foreign. The domestic currency in such countries is commonly over-valued, and maintained through exchange controls, import quotas, and other trade restrictions. The analysis in this chapter is restricted to the use of shadow prices on this interpretation.

2. Since we shall be particularly interested in the shadow, or accounting, prices of imported goods, we shall assume that the official exchange rate of the domestic currency is set at a level other than that which would prevail in conditions of free international trade. If such countries intend to maintain their over-valued currencies through trade and exchange restrictions, in addition to short and long term foreign borrowing, shadow prices are, indeed, indispensable in evaluating projects there. In this connection, some of the largest poor countries come to mind: India, Pakistan, Brazil – although, under a system of fixed exchange rates, West European countries are occasionally prone to periods of trade imbalance which might warrant the introduction of shadow prices.

Assuming full employment and international free trade equilibruim, there is no problem in calculating the accounting price of traded goods. Ignoring transport costs etc., the foreign price of a ton of manganese imported into India is equal to its domestic price there which, in turn, is equal to the value of Indian exports necessary to pay for it. Given perfectly competitive factor and product markets, and the absence of external effects, Indian exports are priced at the opportunity cost of the factors used in their production. In that case the domestic price of a ton of imported manganese (or a unit of any other import) is equal, ultimately, to the opportunity cost of the Indian factors used in producing the goods to pay for it.

Removing the assumption of international free trade, the domestic costs of imports rise with the degree of protection provided. If there is, say, a 200 per cent *ad valorem* tariff on manganese, the domestic price will be three times the foreign or world price (assuming constant world supply price). The question arises, which price do we use – the domestic or the world price – as the relevant opportunity cost of the manganese imports to the Indian economy. The accounting price for Indian exports poses a similar problem. Do we use the world price of such exports[2] or do we use the value of these exports to the domestic economy?

3. There is no question but that if $1 million of foreign exchange can be used to purchase x tons of foreign steel, or y tons of foreign nickel, then, *in terms of exchange reserves*, x tons of foreign steel and y tons of foreign nickel are equally costly irrespective of the duties on each. The revenues from the tariffs can, of course, be regarded simply as transfer payments, the cost (in terms of foreign exchange) to the country, as a consumer in the world economy, being simply the world price—assuming, always, that it is constant.[3]

One may concede all this, however, without concluding, that in any cost-benefit study, traded goods should be valued at world prices. On the contrary, there may be a stronger case to be made for valuing traded goods at domestic prices. We shall be in a better position to say so after some analysis of the conditions under which either sort of valuation is allocatively correct.

In general, the question of valuation depends on the relevant political constraints. The economist, as a rule, will accept the rate of exchange as a datum over the foreseeable future, and he will do so in full knowledge of the restrictions on trade and payments that the government deems necessary to maintain it. If, therefore, within the foreseeable future, there is small expectation of any change in existing policy, the economist does the best he can only by working within these apparently irremovable restrictions.[4]

We shall now compare the effects, on the prices of traded goods, of quotas and tariffs under two main assumptions; first (a) that the government cannot further increase its imports by exporting additional goods, but can do so only by reducing other imports; and

[2] The use of world prices in evaluating projects has been recommended most recently by Little and Mirlees (1969).

[3] If the foreign supply price is upward-sloping, the marginal import cost is above the foreign price. (Similarly, if the foreign demand for the country's exports is downward slopping, the country's marginal export revenue is below the foreign demand price.) But since we are concerned here with more fundamental issues, we may assume that over the relevant range world supply prices are constant unless otherwise stated.

[4] The economist may, indeed he should, urge on the authorities the need for a change to more 'rational' economic policies. But once he comes to making cost-benefit estimates, they are to be made with reference to those economic policies that are likely to prevail, not those that 'ought to' prevail.

secondly, (b) that it can increase its imports by increasing its exports, though at increasing cost.

4. (a) Suppose, first, a rigid quota system for manganese imports, having the result that the demestic market price is $3,000 a ton, whereas the foreign purchase price is $1,000 a ton.[5] Since existing private firms value the manganese at $3,000 a ton, a public enterprise, requiring annually 100 tons of manganese that could not make a profit at this price of $3,000 per ton might yet be able to make a profit if it costed the imported manganese at only $1,000 per ton. If this is the case, the manganese allocated by the government to this public project will be at the expense of that used in the private sector. But the resulting movement of a scarce material from existing uses to one where it has a lower value is a retrograde move: potential welfare is reduced.

If, then, no more imports of manganese are permitted we should allow the public enterprise to buy it from the domestic market at the going price of $3,000 a ton which, in these circumstances, is to be entered as the opportunity cost of manganese.

It is, however, quite possible for the government, while maintaining unchanged the *total* foreign exchange value of imports, to reduce some other kind of imports costing $100,000 of its limited holdings of foreign currency in order to enable the country to import 100 additional tons of manganese. If asked to advise which kinds of current imports should be sactificed so as to make available to the public enterprise this additional 100 tons of manganese, the economist would clearly choose to reduce the $100,000 worth of imports having the lowest domestic value—so minimizing the opportunity cost of these manganese imports.

The economist may not be consulted, however, in which case the domestic value of whatever kinds of imports are actually sacrificed for this purpose may well be higher than is necessary. Whatever the domestic value of these forgone imports – say $100,000 worth of English cutlery – it must be regarded as the relevant opportunity cost of importing the 100 tons of manganese. There is also, however, the opportunity cost of withdrawing manganese from the domestic market.

Let us continue to suppose that the domestic value of 100 tons of manganese is $300,000 whereas the domestic value of the cutlery forgone in order to import an additional 100 tons of manganese is

---

[5] Since the exchange rate is taken to be fixed, dollar prices can be used in lieu of rupee prices.

$250,000, then – provided that there are no political constraints operating to prevent the additional manganese imports being used in the private sector – the relevant opportunity cost to the public investment project is to be taken as equal to $300,000, as in the preceding circumstances. For this $300,000 is the value the 100 tons of manganese will fetch on the domestic market, and unless the public project can meet the chosen investment criterion when paying that price for it, the manganese should be sold to the private sector. If, on the other hand, the government forbids the sale of the additional imports of manganese to the private sector the economist must accept the $250,000 domestic value of the cutlery as the opportunity cost of the 100 tons of manganese imports.

Now suppose, instead, that the government has made it clear that if the project is feasible it will pay for the additional 100 tons of manganese by reducing the imports of transistors having a total domestic value of $350,000. The revelant opportunity cost of the manganese to the public project perforce becomes $350,000. For unless the project can meet the appropriate investment criterion with the manganese costed at $350,000, the alternative of not reducing the imports of transistors yields a higher value to the economy.

For cost-benefit calculation, therefore, as in allocative analysis generally, the opportunity cost of an (imported) input – within the given framework of political constraints – is the (highest) loss of social value that has to be incurred elsewhere in the economy in consequence of its use in the project in question.

(b) Consideration of a flexible quota scheme enables us to introduce an alternative possibility: in any year included in the project's cost-benefit period, India *may increase its exports* in order to pay for the additional 100 tons of manganese. The only conditions under which we can now justify using, as the opportunity cost of manganese, its world price of $1,000 a ton are: (1) that the world demand for one or more of India's exports is infinitely elastic, and (2) that there is no purely domestic tax on the exported good.

Now, as the reader will recognize, the prices of exportables can be forced down if more is offered on the world market so that, in general, marginal export revenue, rather than existing export price, should be used. Apart from bilateral dealings, it may be possible to confine an export subsidy to additional sales only. If so, the additional export revenue will be greater than if prices are reduced on all exports of a particular good.

If we use such information to determine the accounting price of *the additional import* of 100 tons of manganese – supposing for the moment that the second condition, no domestic tax on exported goods, is met – we have to ask: what is the reduction in domestic value necessary to fetch an additional $100,000 of foreign exchange in order to pay for the 100 tons of manganese? If the domestic price of jute is $1 per pound but, because of the inelasticity of foreign demand, 250,000 pounds of it has to be exported to fetch $100,000 of foreign exchange, then the domestic value forgone by the jute exports is $250,000.

Of no less importance is the second condition. If, now, the first condition is met (constant export demand price), and the $100,000 of foreign exchange can be obtained simply by exporting 100,000 pounds of jute, the domestic value forgone will be $100,000 only if there is no domestic tax on jute. If, however, there is, say, a 60 per cent *ad valorem* tax on domestic jute, the domestic value of the 100,000 pounds of exported jute is $160,000.

If neither condition is met, recourse to the above figures would involve a loss of domestic value of $250,000 plus 60 per cent, or $400,000—this being the loss of value to the domestic economy experienced by the withdrawal of the 250,000 pounds of jute that are needed to pay for the additional 100 tons of manganese from abroad.

Where either of the first two conditions alone are not met, the loss of domestic value from exporting the necessary amount of jute happens to be below the domestic value of the 100 tons of manganese. Provided that there is no government prohibition on the sales of newly imported manganese to the domestic market, then, in accordance with our definition of opportunity cost, the domestic value of the 100 tons of manganese, or $300,000, has to be regarded as the correct opportunity cost. On the other hand, if the government forbids the sale of the additional 100 tons of manganese to the domestic market, the economist has no alternative but to estimate the opportunity cost of the additional 100 tons of manganese as $250,000 under our first supposition, and $160,000 under our second supposition. Under our third supposition, in which neither condition is met, the opportunity cost of the manganese is $400,000 irrespective of whether the government forbids the domestic sale of the additional manganese imports or not.

Removing the assumption of constant world supply prices can raise the opportunity price of manganese further. For example, let the elasticity of the world supply curve of manganese be such that additional imports of 100 tons per annum involve payment of $200,000—or twice as much foreign exchange as with a constant world supply price, and therefore twice the volume of Indian exports. The opportunity cost of the 100 additional tons of manganese becomes $800,000—being the value to the domestic economy of the loss of 500,000 pounds of jute.[6]

The exposition has been simplified throughout by assuming that small changes in the domestic amounts of importables and exportables have negligible effects on their prices. If this simplification is dropped, the area under the relevant portion of the demand curve has to be substituted as a measure of value rather than domestic price *times* quantity, as used.

---

[6] I have made no allowance in these proposals for the degree of monopoly in the production of the chosen exported good, say, jute. In so far as the domestic price (without tax) of jute is above the export price the argument in the text applies, the relevant price being the domestic price.

It is true that the greater the degree of monopoly (as measured say, by the ratio of price to marginal cost) in the production of jute as compared with the production of other goods in the economy, the greater the scope for allocative improvements. Again, however, though the economist can recommend such improvements, in undertaking a cost-benefit study he has to accept the present and future prices of goods (corrected for spillover effects) as indicative of their value, at the margin, to the community.

CHAPTER 13

Shadow Prices (continued)

1. Let us now shift our attention from quota schemes, or exchange controls (that directly ration either particular categories of imported goods or else imported goods in general), toward tariff schemes that ration imports by price. The essential arguments are unchanged. If there is a 200 per cent *ad valorem* tariff on manganese, a ton of manganese bought at $1,000 on the world market sells at a domestic price of $3,000. True, in the tariff case the government collects the revenue of $2,000 on each imported ton of manganese, whereas in the quota case this $2,000 becomes a windfall to the initial recipient of the quota who might well (if the government allows it) sell his quota-permit to others at a maximum price of $2,000 per permitted ton. But whether this 'monopoly rent' is received by the government, or by private persons or firms, is merely a distributional aspect which, of itself, provides no guidance in the determination of the accounting price of imported manganese. What is again significant, however, is the potential sacrifice of domestic value entailed in using an additional ton of manganese for this project. Where the country cannot, or will not, increase its exports, the opportunity cost of 100 tons of manganese is, as before, either the domestic value of manganese or else (if valued higher) the domestic value of those imported goods that are to be withdrawn from the economy in order to make available the foreign exchange for the manganess imports. Where the country is able, and chooses, to pay for the additional manganese by additional exports, its opportunity cost is the domestic value subtracted from the economy by exporting goods in order to meet the additional foreign payments.

More generally, the import of an additional 100 tons of manganese, presents the country with a choice of reducing other imports, or increasing exports, or a combination of both.

It goes without saying that, accepting the existing trade restrictions, economic efficiency is promoted by keeping the opportunity costs of either method in line with one another. If the smallest loss of domestic value from reducing other kinds of imports were $300,000, and the smallest loss of domestic value from increasing exports were $350,000, the first method – import-reduction – is to be preferred each time until both methods (or any combination of the two methods) yield the same result. Again, however, the economist can only recommend such policies to the government. In so far as the government fails to implement them, the economist must derive his social costing from the actual, or expected, responses. If the government elects to pay for an additional 100 tons of manganese by additional exports of jute, which subtract from the economy a domestic value of $400,000, when it might instead have raised the necessary foreign exchange by exports of raw cotton, which would subtract a domestic value of $300,000, the actual accounting cost of the manganese continues to be $400,000 until such time as the government changes its policy and makes payment through cotton exports.

2.   So much for the calculation of accounting prices for *imports* used in public projects. What of the calculation of accounting prices for the *exported* outputs of these projects? It will be conceded that goods produced by the project, and exported, should be evaluated by reference to the same conceptual framework used in determining the accounting prices of imports. But the public project's imports, regarded as alternatives to the use of domestic inputs, are valued as opportunity costs,[1] whereas exports of the project's output, regarded as alternative to domestic consumption, are valued as social benefits. The measure of such benefits is the value to the domestic economy of the imports they make available to it.[2] In particular, the benefit measure of the project's exports is the domestic value of the specific goods that will be imported from the additional foreign exchange made available. A rational procedure, in this connection, would be one that used the additional exchange reserves in purchasing imports having the largest domestic value—account being taken of external effects, if any. But, again, in any project evaluations the calculation of the expected benefits, arising from the project's exports, must depend on the economist's judgment of the additional imports the government will actually allow; if one million yards of cloth exported by a new textile project adds $1 million to the foreign exchange reserves, they should not be priced at $1 million but at the domestic value of the additional imports that are to be bought for the $1 million. Given, say, a rising foreign supply price for the imports in

[1]   The costs of these imports can, if necessary, be compared directly with the benefit to be imputed to them from the sale of the outputs of the project – ultimately the addition to domestic social value.

[2]   The benefits of the exports, so calculated, can also be compared directly with the costs of their production – ultimately their opportunity cost in terms of domestic value forgone.

question (which reduces the buying power of the extra $1 million foreign exchange) and a high tariff on those imports, the domestic value of the additional imports, now made possible by these exports, could be, say, $2,500,000, which is then the social benefit, or accounting price, of the additional exports of cloth.[3]

In sum, the accounting prices of both additional imports and exports involved in any investment project – or the social opportunity cost of imports and the social benefits of exports – are to be calculated by reference respectively to the subtraction from, and addition to, the country's domestic value, not by reference to world prices of traded goods.

Admittedly the implementing of these proposals will present more difficulty than the use of world prices as accounting prices. For one thing, the practising economist cannot always be sure, in evaluating a project involving traded goods, which particular imports will be displaced, or which particular imports or exports will be increased. He has, perforce, to engage in some guesswork. But he is at least guessing at the magnitudes of the right things. And wherever the calculations that arise from using two alternative methods can be significantly different – as they certainly can be wherever substantial trade restrictions exist – it is advisable to place reliance upon rough estimates of the relevant concepts than on more exact estimates of irrelevant ones.

[3] It might seem reasonable to argue that the exportable part of the output of the project *also* has an *opportunity cost*, in that it could have been sold instead on the home market and added, therefore to domestic value. Again, however, the resolution of the problem depends upon the constraints postulated. If the economist is to decide where all the project's outputs are to go, in particular which parts are to be exported and which retained for home use, he will regard them as alternative opportunities and, therefore, choose to place any output where it adds most to domestic value. In the text, however, we are assuming that the decision to export certain portions of the project's annual output is one that has already been made either by authority or custom, or possibly by the economist working within certain constraints.

CHAPTER 14

Some Limitations of Partial Analysis

1. It is commonplace knowledge that the optimal conditions that guide allocative decisions are no more than first order, or necessary conditions in maximizing a social welfare function subject to a production constraint.[1] The second-best theorem (Lipsey and Lancaster, 1957) does no more than point out that, if one or more additional constraints are imposed on this welfare function, the necessary conditions for a maximum are different from the usual ones and, in general, are more complex. The obvious corollary follows that, in order to identify a maximum welfare position under these circumstances, it may be necessary to forsake those familiar optimal conditions that are strictly relevant to the simple case of a single constraint, the boundary of production possibilities.

Now in the simple case of no constraint additional to the production boundary, the more relevant set of necessary conditions is cast in the familiar form of setting the price of each good proportional to its corresponding marginal cost. Put otherwise, the ratio of the prices of any pair of goods has to be made equal to the ratio of their corresponding marginal costs. It follows, therefore, that if there is but one constraint additional to the production boundary, which takes the form, say, of the price in sector X being 40 per cent above its marginal cost, the above condition is met – and a general optimal position attained – simply by setting the prices in all the remaining sectors 40 per cent above their corresponding marginal costs.

One cannot depend on the problem being that simple, however, and the economist has to face the question of determining a price and output for one or more industries in circumstances where he cannot hope to influence price and output policies in the rest of the economy. Since there is not the slightest prospect of his being able to obtain the necessary data to calculate an exact second-best solution for the industry, or industries, in question, it is necessary to consider conditions under which he can, with some assurance, recommend either marginal cost pricing or some other simple rule.

[1] The reader may wish to consult my *Survey of Welfare Economics* (1960), Section II, for an interpretation and critical examination of these optimal conditions.

The existence of varying degrees of monopoly in the economy at large does not, of itself, justify much concern over misallocation. Enterprises that continue to survive are able to cover their full costs and, in a fairly competitive economy, not many enterprises are likely to make revenues that vastly exceed their costs for any length of time. Thus, although it is not to be expected that the economy, at any moment of time, attains an optimum position, in its continuous adjustment to changes in the conditions of demand and supply, it may not be too far from an overall optimal position for any prolonged period.[2]

The one factor that diminishes such hopes, however, even in a highly competitive economy, is the existence of significant spillover effects, since there is no necessary tendency here towards self-correction. The larger the spillover effects and the less uniform is their incidence throughout the economy, the smaller is the confidence that can be reposed in the presumption that a competitive economy tends to a tolerably good allocation.[3]

However, in so far as the economist is not addressing himself to general policies designed to improve overall allocation in the economy but is, instead, restricting himself to evaluation of some specific project that is technically feasible, he need not be too inhibited by the second-best theorem. For no matter what the allocative condition of the economy at large, a Pareto improvement is effected if a factor is transferred from its existing employment to one where its value is higher – or, put more generally, if the value of the marginal product of the factor to be employed in X exceeds its opportunity cost.[4]

[2] The scope for improvement in productive, or technological, efficiency may, however, be far more important than allocative efficiency of this overall sort. And if so, the question of whether to spend a given sum of money in seeking such allocative improvements or in seeking advances in productive efficiency is easily answered. But whether attempts at increasing productive efficiency are successful or not, the allocative problem still remains.

For the arguments that productivity improvements are, at present, more profitable than the usual allocative improvements, the reader is referred to Leibenstein's 1966 paper.

[3] Allocative and other aspects of spillovers, and their treatment in a cost-benefit analysis, are discussed at length in Part III which follows.

[4] In general, any transfer of factors from one product to another affects the distribution of real earnings in the economy, and also the relative prices of the goods as between which factors are transferred, both of these consequences affecting the general pattern of demand, and, therefore, the existing price-marginal cost ratios. The first feature in particular implies that the optimal position itself – uniquely determined only if there is a uniquely specified welfare function (which, in fact, is usually assumed in the treatment of second-best theory)

2.   Turning to the question of marginal cost pricing – either in the long run, which determines the size of the plant, or in the short run, which determines the output produced by the existing plant – the reader is reminded that the question has been discussed under the tacit assumption that any necessary changes in the tax structure do not, of themselves, have any allocative effects.

In the long period the optimal size of the plant is determined by the condition that demand price equals long period marginal cost. If, therefore, the demand curve cuts the long-period marginal cost curve at an output in the range of declining average cost – marginal cost, and therefore price, being below average cost – the plant size will be one for which average (inclusive) cost is below price. And if there is only one price, set to equal marginal cost, the enterprise cannot meet its total cost from its revenues. Similarly, if, in the short period, the demand is such that the output for which price equals marginal cost is one for which marginal cost is below average cost, the marginal cost pricing rule specifies an output at which, so priced, total revenues fall short of total factor costs.[5]

By discriminating monopoly pricing or, more practically, by the use of two- or multi-part tariffs, the marginal cost-pricing rule can, however, be made consistent with the aim of covering the full costs of the enterprise.[6] There may, however, be political or other constraints that rule out the possibility of two- or multi-part tariffs. If so, the alternative is either (a) that of producing a smaller than optimal output in order to cover costs – setting price equal, at least, to average cost (and, therefore, above marginal cost) – or else (b) that

---

– alters in response to the factor movements which one would want to recommend by reference to the marginal cost price ratios of the existing situation. Nonetheless, in so far as the magnitudes of the factor movements are those pertinent to cost-benefit studies, the assumptions of partial analysis may be adopted, for the secondary repercussions on product prices arising from such relatively limited factor movements are likely to be negligible.

5   The reader is reminded that the marginal cost pricing condition is a necessary, but not sufficient, condition. Confining ourselves to a partial analysis, it is required also that total benefit from the output exceeds total costs.

6   A two-part tariff is usually one which exacts a fixed charge from the buyer unrelated to the amount of the good he takes at the price. The commonest examples are quarterly charges for telephone service and for electricity service, which charges are set independently of the consumption of the services. Such charges have the effect of transferring a portion of what would otherwise be the consumers surplus to the service enterprises.

of subsidizing the enterprise so as to enable it to meet its factor payments when it sets a price equal to marginal cost (and, therefore, below average cost).

If there are no 'distortions' involved in raising taxes – as, in principle, there would not be if lump-sum taxes could be levied[7] – there can be no purely *allocative* objections to the (b) alternative and, therefore, to financing a falling-cost service by means of a public subsidy. But raising additional taxes of the usual sort does involve the community in costs. Apart from additional administrative costs of altering the tax structure, and of collecting the taxes, the raising of taxes, other than lump-sum taxes, has incidental allocative effects. Income taxes, in particular, can have effects on effort, and can reduce the incentive to produce marketable goods or services while increasing the incentive to spend more time and effort in evading taxes. In view of these income tax effects, there may be a case, after all, for setting price above marginal cost and equal to average cost. The consequent misallocation need not be serious if the prices of substitutes for this good are already set somewhat above their corresponding marginal costs and/or the demand for this good has a low elasticity.

There may, also, be political or social objections, which the economist has to accept, to pricing a good at its marginal cost in the long or short period, and financing the loss through public subsidies. If the good was consumed predominantly by wealthier groups, distributive arguments could be brought against the proposal to price at marginal cost and cover the losses from public revenues. On the other hand, even if the revenues raised by marginal cost pricing sufficed, or more than sufficed, to meet factor payments, there may also be objections to it on distributive grounds. It is not, for example, impractical to charge public transit passengers different fares for travelling at different times of the day. During peak-traffic hours, at least, higher fares could be charged to meet the higher marginal (congestion) costs. But, it may be objected, the passengers during peak hours have little choice in view of traditional business hours. In the circumstances, charging according to marginal costs would be charging lower income groups more for having to travel in discomfort, compared with those who have the choice and the leisure

[7] Lump sum taxes are taken to mean taxes that are invariant to a person's earnings. Although, as a result of the wealth effect, such taxes will in general alter the supply of a person's productive services, they will not 'distort' the objective rate of substitution between factor and product. If, therefore, there are no other taxes in the economy, the introduction of lump-sum taxes does not infringe the factor-product optimal condition. If lump sum taxes are not feasible, a second-best tax system can be devised. See Baumol and Bradford (1970).

to travel more comfortably at other hours. This is so manifestly inequitable[8] that it has not been seriously contemplated. In such cases, then, political constraints translate marginal cost pricing into 'average' marginal cost pricing.[9] And if public subsidy is not forthcoming, there may be no choice but to resort to 'average' average cost pricing.

References and Bibliography for Part II

Blaug, M., 'The Rate of Return on Investment in Education in Great Britain', *The Manchester School*, 1965.

Borus, M. E., 'A Benefit Cost Analysis of the Economic Effectiveness of Retraining the Unemployed', *Yale Economic Essays*, 1964.

Dorfman, R. (ed.), *Measuring the Benefit of Government Investments*, Washington D.C.: Brookings Institution, 1965 (London: Allen & Unwin's, 1968).

Eckstein, O., *Water Resource Development*, Cambridge, Mass. Harvard University Press, 1958.

Hammond, R. J., *Benefit-Cost Analysis and Water Pollution Control*, Stanford: University Press, 1958.

Hansen, W. L., 'Total and Private Rates of Return to Investment in Schooling', *Journal of Political Economy*, 1963.

Haveman, R. H. and Krutilla, J. V., *Unemployment, Idle Capacity, and the Evaluation of Public Expenditure*, Washington, D.C.: Resources for the Future, Inc., 1968.

Hicks, J. R., *A Revision of Demand Theory*, Oxford: Clarendon Press, 1956.

Leibenstein, H., 'Allocative Efficiency versus X-Efficiency', *American Economic Review*, 1966.

Lipsey, R. and Lancaster, K., 'The General Theory of Second Best', *Review of Economic Studies*, 1957.

Little, I. M. D. and Mirrlees, J., *Social Cost Benefit Analysis*. Paris, 1969.

McKean, R. N., *Efficiency in Government Through Systems Analysis*, London: Wiley, 1958.

Mishan, E. J., 'Survey of Welfare Economics, 1939–1959', *Economic Journal*, 1960.

———— 'Interpretation of the Benefits of Private Transport', *Journal of Transport Economics and Policy*, 1967.

———— 'What is Producer's Surplus?', *American Economic Review*, 1968.

———— *Cost-Benefit Analysis* (2nd edn), London: Allen & Unwin, 1975.

Mohring. H., 'Land Values and the Measurement of Highway Benefits', *Journal of Political Economy*, 1961.

Mushkin, Selma J., 'Health as an Investment', *Journal of Political Economy*, 1962. •

Peters, G. H., *Cost-Benefit Analysis and Public Expenditure*, London: Institute of Economic Affairs, 1968.

[8] For a useful discussion of the role and feasibility of marginal cost pricing, the reader should consult Vickrey's 1955 paper.

[9] If vehicular traffic is believed to be subsidized, inasmuch as its current operational marginal costs do not include the spillover effects it generates, there is a case for setting the public transit fares below marginal costs.

Prest, A. R. and Turvey, R., 'Cost-Benefit Analysis: A Survey', *Economic Journal*, 1965.

Rothenberg, J., 'Urban Renewal Programs' in R. Dorfman (ed.), *Measuring the Benefits of Government Investment*, Washington D.C.: Brookings Institution, 1965 (London: Allen & Unwin, 1968).

Throsby, D., *An Introduction to Mathematical Programming*, New York: Random House, 1970.

Vickrey, W., 'Some Implications of Marginal Cost Pricing for Public Utilities', *American Economic Review* (Supplement), 1955.

Weisbrod, B. A., *Economics of Public Health; Measuring the Impact of Diseases*, Philadelphia: University of Philadelphia Press, 1960.

Winch, D. M., *The Economics of Highway Planning*, Toronto: Toronto University Press, 1963.

Wiseman, J., 'The Theory of Public Utility Price—An Empty Box', *Oxford Economic Papers*, 1957.

CHAPTER 15

What are External Effects?

1. What are now known in the jargon as external effects, or spillover or side effects, first appear in Alfred Marshall's *Principles* (1925) in connection with a competitive industry's downward sloping supply curve. Using today's economic parlance, Marshall's argument can be paraphrased as follows – assume, for simplicity of exposition, that all the firms in the industry are equally efficient. An expansion of the competitive industry by, say, a single firm lowers the average cost of production to *all* the firms in the industry including this new firm. Since the total reduction of costs experienced by all the intra-marginal firms is to be attributed to the entry of this additional firm, the true cost of its additional output is *not* the total cost as calculated by that firm, but this total cost *less* the savings in total costs experienced by all the intra-marginal firms. If, therefore, firms continue to enter the competitive industry until, at the going price of the product, the total cost of each of the firms is equal to its total revenue, the long period equilibruim size of the industry will, as we know, be that at which the market demand price is equal to the average (inclusive) cost of the good in question, with each firm making zero profit. But, in the case where the industry's supply curve falls as more is produced, the true total cost of the incremental firm, and therefore also its true average and marginal cost, are below those it calculates since its calculations take no account of the savings in cost it confers on all intra-marginal firms. It follows, therefore, that its true average, and marginal cost will be, to that extent, below the market price and, abiding by the marginal-cost pricing rule, output has to be extended beyond the competitive equilibruim until the true marginal cost is equal to price. The existence of external economies in a competitive industry, we conclude, entails an equilibruim output that is below optimal.

Constructing a curve marginal to the industry's supply curve, the point at which this marginal curve cuts the demand curve identifies the 'ideal', or optimal, output. This concept, and its corresponding construction, was extended in a symmetrical manner to external diseconomies, to reveal that the optimal output of a competitive industry was below the equilibruim output. These external effects were later remarked to have wide application, not only as between firms in determining the optimal size of the industry, but as between industries themselves; nor are such effects confined to industry. They operate as between persons and groups, and as between firms and industries and persons.

2. Familiar examples today of spillover effects include the adverse effects on flora, fauna, rainfall, and soil, in cutting down the trees of a forest; or the effects on the mosquito population of creating artificial lakes, and other ecological repercussions that ultimately touch upon the welfare of people. The pleasure given by the erection of a beautiful building or, more commonly alas, the offence given by the erection of a tasteless or incongruous structure, is an external effect. So also is the congestion suffered by all the traffic from additional vehicles coming onto the roads; or the noise and pollution arising from the operation of industry or of its products; or the loss of life consequent upon the increase in air or ground traffic.

From a little reflection on examples such as these, it emerges that one characteristic common to all of them is the incidental, or unintentional nature of the effect produced. The person or industrial concern engaged, say, in logging may, or may not, have any idea of the consequences on the profits or welfare of others. But it is certain that they do not enter into his calculations. The factory owners, whose plant produces smoke as well as other things, are concerned only to produce the other things that can be sold on the market. They have no interest in producing smoke, even though they may be fully aware of it. But so long as their own productivity does not suffer thereby, and they themselves are not penalized in any way, they will regard the smoke as an unfortunate by-product.

If these external effects are not deliberately produced, however, neither are they deliberately absorbed by others. Such effects may add to the enjoyment of life, as does the smell of fresh-cut grass, or else add to life's vexations as does the noise, stench, and danger of mounting automobile traffic. But they are not within the control of the persons who are absorbing them – at least not without their incurring expenses.[1] However, a definition of external effects that gives prominence to these aspects – that a person's welfare, or a firm's

---

[1] If an adverse spillover effect could be avoided without incurring any costs, it could hardly be called an adverse spillover. Certainly no problem would arise.

profits, depend upon things that are initially outside his control, which things are incidental to the activity of others – is by itself insufficient and may, indeed, lead to confusion. Let us see how.

3. The statement that a firm's or industry's outputs or profits, or a person's welfare, can be influenced by the activities of others is true, apparently, within the context of any general equilibruim system. In particular, it is true within a general equilibruim system that has no external effects of the sort illustrated above.[2] The familiar inter-dependent system of Leon Walras is a case in point. Among the set of equations posited are those for individuals regarded as consumers and owners of productive services. All the *variables* in each person's utility function – whether they refer to the amounts of finished goods bought or the amounts of productive services offered – are deemed to be entirely within his control. The parameters within each person's utility function, however, are the set of prices; and these are determined by the system as a whole.

Thus for each person, the quantities of the things that he is willing to buy or to sell depends, *interalia*, on the set of market prices of these things. The amounts of goods supplied by perfectly competing firms also depend upon the market prices. These sets of market prices can, in general, be altered by any changes in technology, in people's tastes, or in the accumulation and redistribution of assets. It follows that the activities of persons and firms, in response to these sorts of changes, have incidental effects on the welfare of others. If, to take a humble example, people start changing from tea to coffee, the price of tea will at first tend to fall and that of coffee to rise. The producers of tea will initially suffer and those of coffee benefit, while the consumers of tea will be better off and the consumers of coffee worse off.

But in this general equilibrium system, in the absence of all external effects as commonly understood, such interdependence operates indirectly, and through changes in market prices. Each and every exogenous change mentioned – a change in techniques, in tastes, or in factor endowment – entails a corresponding change in the equilibrium set of prices. Since, in general, every price is affected, every person's welfare is affected also, and this can be very impor-tant.[3] Nevertheless, given perfectly competitive markets and no

[2] The system is, of course, a *theoretical* construct only. Engineers affirm that in all input-output activites there is wastage, and therefore waste material is absorbed into the air, the earth or its waters, so creating the potential for external effects.

[3] For instance in appraising welfare criteria. See my 1957 paper.

external effects, each general equilibrium position meets the requirements of a Pareto optimum, viz. one in which it is not possible to make one or more persons better off without making at least one person worse off.[4] In contrast, the concern with external effects arises just because their existence implies that – unless special arrangements are made – the equilibrium solutions attainable may *not* be Pareto optimal.

We may, then, infer that external effects are effects on others that are conveyed *directly*, and not indirectly through prices. If we allow that these effects on people's welfare matter in principle no less than do the priced products and services, it follows that it is just because these external effects, these by-products of the activities of others, are not properly priced or not priced at all, that the equilibrium solution is not Pareto optimal. To illustrate, the competitive equilibrium price of steel spades is $10, the price being equal to long-run average, and marginal cost. In their production, however, noise is produced, this being the only external effect in the economy. The noise created in producing the marginal spade would be tolerated without complaint only on receipt of, say, $7 by those disturbed by the noise. The net valuation of the marginal spade is, therefore, $10 minus $7, or $3 altogether. However, the marginal cost is $10, and the equilibrium is not optimal. For if we produced one spade less to start with, the factors released would – assuming universal perfect competition – create $10 of goods elsewhere. The accompanying loss in social value, however, is $3, as above. Society is better off to the extent of $7: some can be made better off (to the extent of $7) without any one else being made worse off. As stated, therefore, the original position could not have been optimal.

If external effects could somehow be 'properly' priced like the other goods and 'bads' of the economic system – where the term 'bads' is occasionally used as an alternative expression to disutility, or 'diswelfare', or 'discommodity', of which, say, the provision of labour services could be taken as an example – then indeed any perfectly competitive equilibruim would, again, be optimal. One can go further: if each external effect were to be priced in a competitive market, along with other goods and bads, it would cease to be an external effect.

4. It emerges, then, that one characteristic of an external effect is that it is not under the control of the person who experiences such

---

[4] If every relevant effect in the economy is properly priced, the economy is in an optimal position. The reverse however is not true, since optimality can be consistent with unpriced spillovers.

effects whether good or bad. Another characteristic is that the external effect is *not* deemed to be a *deliberate* creation of its producer but an incidental, or unintended, by-product of apparently legitimate economic activity. Thus it may be that my wealthy aunt's welfare (as well as my own) depends unambiguously on the amount of arsenic I put into her tea. If it was discovered that in my impatience to inherit her fortunes I had used arsenic to accelerate the natural process of ageing, the coroner would be unlikely to refer to the results of my enterprise as an external effect. Yet, if person 1 be my aunt, person 2 be myself, x_i^2 be the amount of arsenic that I use, $\partial U^1/\partial x_i^2 < 0$ expresses the proposition that my aunt's welfare varies inversely with the amount of arsenic that I use. It would therefore fit the situation just depicted. In contrast, the conventional interpretation of the external effect indicated by the term $\partial U^1/\partial x_i^2 < 0$ would be that my good aunt suffers from my injudicious consumption of arsenic, in small doses, as a stimulant. In order, therefore, to comply with the conventional meaning of external effect, the x_i^2 notation is to be interpreted strictly as person 2's consumption, or production, of good x_i which is determined solely by reference to his own immediate interest, and in disregard of the effects it may have on the welfare of others.

5. Once the reader has a clear idea of what an external effect is,[5] a little reflection will convince him that the number of external effects in the real world are virtually unlimited. If my wife is envious of her friend's new fur coat, her friend's wearing it in my wife's presence has an adverse external effect on at least one person. A cigar smoked in the presence of non-smokers has adverse external effects. Attractive short-skirted women may generate adverse external effects on

[5] There are quite a number of economic phenomena – all, perhaps, relevant to considerations of optimality – masquerading in the literature as external effects which cannot be admitted on the interpretation in the text. Common among these are such developments as better information (especially about the investment plans of others), the pooling of risks, improved training facilities, and other cost-saving arrangements. Such arbitrary extensions of the original concept, and the consequent ambiguity generated, are discussed in my 1965 paper. A recent misapprehension arises in the case of a person who cannot be admitted into an already packed theatre, or who has to queue without certainty of entry. The consequent decline in his welfare, certainly related to the welfare of others, is not, however, an instance of external effects, but of non-optimal pricing. An ideal mechanism would choose a set of prices as to fill the theatre exactly (ignoring discontinuities), with no one left out who would be willing to pay the price to get in. There are, of course, obvious practical difficulties in implementing such an 'optimal' set of prices; and these, not external effects, account for these frustrations.

other women and favourable external effects on men. A's promotion causes B to rejoice, and C to curse. And so one could go on.

Now if all the administrative costs, and all the associated expenses and efforts involved in reaching mutually satisfactory arrangements were zero, the possibilities for mutual gain would be completely exhausted and, by definition, a Pareto optimum would prevail. Thinking along such lines, the utilitarian (in the narrow sense) would approve of measures designed to reduce the cost of reaching mutual agreements about external effects. If, for example, negligible time and effort are required for the non-smoker to bribe the smoker to desist from lighting his cigarette, both can be made better off by the arrangement. However, the potential gains of a vast number of such mutual arrangements are likely to be smaller than the minimal costs and efforts needed for such arrangements. They are uneconomic in the sense that once these costs and efforts enter the calculus, the net potential benefits are negative.

But this is not all. Not all the external effects for which some arrangements would reveal net potential benefits that are positive are socially acceptable. Economists, and society at large, might wish to distinguish, and in practice do distinguish, between external effects that are a source of 'legitimate' satisfaction or grievance, and those that are not. Among the latter are the resentment or envy felt by some people at the achievement or possessions of others.[6] But though such reactions may elicit sympathy, and qualify for psychiatry, they are unlikely to command moral approval. Once ethics are brought into external effects in this way, the question of which effects are to count and which not must, in the last resort, depend upon a consensus in the particular society. Though such ethical distinctions will confine the application of Pareto improvements to 'legitimate' external effects, the economist would appear justified in accepting a distinction that society consistently makes. Though perhaps not formally embodied in legal documents, no economic policy that caters to these 'negative feelings' of people has ever been announced. In contrast, there is no lack of evidence that society does take seriously all tangible damage inflicted on some people by others in their pursuit of pleasure or profit. Since adverse environmental effects provide, today, the most important instances of damage inadvertently inflicted on other people, they will feature prominently in our discussion on methods of evaluating them.

[6] These are sometimes referred to as 'interdependence effects', since they are conceived of as the utility of one person being dependent upon the utility of another person – either directly, or via the goods that enter into the other's utility function.

CHAPTER 16

Internalizing External Effects

1. The nature of an external effect may be considered further by examining the concept of 'internalizing' it. The basic idea is that of transforming the external effect, or incidental by-product, into a joint product. Before the turn of the century, cattle were slain in Argentina for their leather only. Their flayed carcasses were left to rot, but if found in time they could be used as fresh meat by the poor peasants. Apparently only the leather had a market price, the meat being a by-product, or external effect, of leather production—a favourable spillover of the leather industry for those peasants who happened to be in the vicinity.[1]

Suppose, however, that the human population began to multiply more rapidly than the cattle population, that the taste for meat grew, that meat began to be stored in refrigerators and that, most important of all perhaps, the meat could be exported to distant markets. Domestic meat would become scarce and, therefore, a market for it would come into being. It would then cease to be a spillover, an unintended by-product in the process of obtaining hides for leather. It would take its place as a good in its own right, a joint product with leather. Whatever the separate demands for meat and leather are like, the long run competitive equilibrium output is optimal since the cattle population is expanded to the point at which the sum of the market prices is equal to the marginal cost of cattle production. The external effect has been internalized into the pricing system.[2]

---

[1] Notwithstanding which, the number of cattle slain could be optimal if, at the margin, the value of the meat was zero. We discuss this point further in the next chapter in terms of "allocative significance'.

[2] It may seen unnecessary to remark that the possibility of internalizing an external effect (or, in the absence of internalization, correcting for optimal outputs), does not mean that the creation of an adverse external effect need not make things worse. Yet students do sometimes argue as though this is so; as though, so long as optimizing by one method or another takes place, the creation of adverse external effects may be viewed with equanimity. The introduction of an adverse external effect into the economy is a bad thing no matter how the economy adapts to it. By internalizing the bad, or by optimizing the output that produces the bad, we are doing no more than making the best of a bad job. We are certainly not as well off as we should be if this bad had not appeared on the economic scene.

The internalizing of spillover effects also arises in the case of external diseconomies that are internal to the industry. Common examples of the latter category are deep-sea fishing, in which any additional fishing boat above a certain number reduces the catch of each of the existing fishing boats in the fishing grounds; or traffic congestion, in which every additional vehicle above a certain number causes delay to each of the existing number of vehicles using a given highway system. Internalizing this sort of spillover would require that a positive market price be imputed to the currently unpriced though scarce resource – the area of the sea in the first case, the highway in the second. Once such a resource is priced, it will be used more economically. The analogy of scarce land used in the production of, say, corn is exact. If priced correctly, which implies that in a competitive industry the rent of this scarce resource be maximized, the competitive equilibrium output that emerges is also the optimal output.[3]

Another example, though one in which internal accounting prices are substituted for market prices, is that of two separately owned but adjacent factories, A and B. Factory A produces shoes and is powered by an old-fashioned coal engine which emits so much smoke as to seriously affect the output of the B factory, which produces chocolate bars. The manager of the B factory remonstrates with the A manager, but to no effect. The daughter of the owner of the A factory and the son of the owner of the B factory decide to get married, in consequence of which the two factories come under common ownership and control, and the couple live together happily ever after. The cost of the smoke, reckoned in terms of the damage inflicted on the output of the B factory, is no longer a spillover generated by A and suffered by B. It is now unambiguously a cost to the joint A–B enterprise and, as such, ways and means of reducing it will be sought. Either anti-smoke devices will be installed in the A factory, or else, if cheaper (and assuming the smoke-damage to B's output varies directly with A's output) A's output will be reduced to the point at which the value of the marginal damage to B's output, added to the marginal cost of shoe-production in A, is equal to the market price of A's shoes. Thus the smoke ceases to become a spillover effect, but a

---

[3] Assuming a period during which there is one scarce fixed factor and one factor that is variable in supply at a constant price, the average cost curve eventually slopes upward. A curve drawn marginal to this average cost curve cuts the demand curve at the optimal output. At this output, the difference between average cost and marginal cost *times* output gives the amount of the rent to the fixed factor – the maximum rent possible in a perfectly competitive market in which the price of the product is treated as a parameter.

properly costed item that is internalized into the costing system of the
$A-B$ merger.

2. The number of spillover effects that can be internalized into the
pricing mechanism or into the costing systems of firms, is, however,
limited. Among those that cannot be internalized are many of the
by-products of modern industry and the hardware it produces. One
thinks, in this connection, of noise and various forms of pollution
arising from the spread of sewage, garbage and radioactive wastes;
also of the phenomenal postwar growth of diseases of the nerves,
heart, and stomach, caused by high-tension living, the most ubiqui-
tous by-product of sustained technological advance. Why cannot
such spillovers be internalized? The answer is simple: in order that
a competitive market for such spillovers may emerge, certain
conditions have to be met which, in the nature of the physical universe, cannot be met. Firstly, the potential victim of these adverse
spillover effects must have legal 'property rights' in, say, their ownership of some quantum of quiet and clean air which, if such rights
were enjoyed, they could choose to sell to others. Secondly, in order
for such rights to be enforceable, it would be necessary to demarcate
a three-dimensional 'territory' about the person of each potential
victim in order to identify the intrusions of others and take appropriate legal action. Thirdly, in order for a monopolistic situation
not to arise, each of these three-dimensional properties within a given
area, which can be rented for particular purposes (say, to accom-
modate the noise or pollution of someone's activity), must be a close
substitute for the others.

The first condition could, of course, be met in the sense that all
forms of pollution could be outlawed in the absence of specific agreements between the parties concerned. But because the second condition cannot be met in the world we inhabit, there is difficulty in
demarcating each person's property, and a consequent difficulty in
identifying the trespasser and the extent of the trespass. Nor can the
third condition be met, for in this hypothetical scheme of things the
right to use one man's 'territory', within some given area, is no
substitute for that of another man. Each man within the area has his
own three-dimensional territory and, since the noise to be created
by the new activity enters in some degree into all of such territories,
the enterprise has to reach agreement with each one of them. None
can substitute for the other. Unless all agree, the permission of
those who do is worthless.

If it were otherwise, if one territory could be substituted freely for
another, as could plots of land in an agricultural area, an appropriate

market price would arise from the competition of the sellers. The physical universe being what it is, however, each potential seller is in a completely monopolistic position. For without his particular consent the necessary arrangement for the whole of the affected area cannot be concluded. The reader will detect a similarity between this hypothetical problem, posed by the third condition, and that facing a railroad company having to buy every mile of land through which the track has to run. The cost of acquiring rights where a large number of landowners are involved could be prohibitive were it not for legislation compelling the sale of rights on terms which the courts will decide are reasonable. Another instance, occasionally reported by the press, is that of a single householder, or small business, holding out against a property company that is attempting to buy up a specific area of land as part of some new development scheme.

We must, then, resign ourselves to the prospect of never being able to internalize these important environmental spillovers within the economy: that is, of not being able to create a market for them—which is, of course, one of the reasons why cost-benefit methods are required to evaluate them.

3. Some further light is cast on the nature of spillover effects by briefly observing the connection between them and collective, or public, goods. Environmental spillovers usually affect a large number of people within an area. If the spillover effect is favourable, it can be regarded as a form of collective good; if unfavourable, as a form of collective bad. If the favourable spillover effect is to be distinguished from a collective good, it is simply on the grounds (1) that the spillover is only a by-product of some other market-oriented activity, whereas the collective good is itself the intended product, and (2) that an adverse spillover effect, at least, is commonly thought of as *unavoidable*, or avoidable only at a cost, whereas the collective good may well be avoidable. To illustrate (2), consider an instance of an avoidable collective good: each person living within a neighbourhood is free to spend his time gazing at the public fountain, or walking in the municipal park.[4] In contrast, a downfall of artificial rain, caused by seeding the clouds above a certain area of farmland, would be an example of an *unavoidable* collective good (or avoidable only at a cost). If, on the other hand, too much rain-water was one of the *by-products* of the destruction of a forest by a lumber company, this adverse spillover could also be regarded as an unavoidable collective bad.

[4] There can, however, be a problem of congestion if the number of people increases relative to the number, or the size, of the facilities provided.

In connection with the deliberately produced collective project whose effects are unavoidable, or non-optional, it must be realized that some persons may, indeed, receive too much of it—which is to say that their marginal valuation of the benefit is negative. Too much artificial rain, for example, might damage the particular crops of certain farmers. One may, nevertheless, call it a collective good if the sum of the maximum amounts of those who, on balance, benefit from the unavoidable collective effect exceeds the minimum payments necessary to compensate those who, on balance, suffer losses.[5] As indicated, one has only to think of this rainfall as one of the incidental effects of some other deliberate activity (the felling of the trees of a forest, or regular airline flights) to place it within the category of spillover effects.

[5] Among those who *on balance* gain from the given artificial rainfall, there can be those farmers whose crops receive too much rain in the sense that the benefit to them of the marginal inch of rain is negative. The optimal condition, however, requires that rain be increased until the sum of the aggregate benefits and losses of the marginal inch of rain is equal to the cost of producing it.

CHAPTER 17

Evaluating External Effects

1. Any particular external effect, or spillover effect, associated with a given project is but one among any number of consequences affecting the welfare of different people in the community. We must consider, therefore, only the *difference* made to their welfare by the spillover effect in question. Any ith person made better off on balance by the spillover effect would offer a maximum positive sum, V_i, rather than go without it, such sum being prefixed by a positive sign. Any ith person made worse off on balance would require some minimum sum V_i to induce him to put up with the spillover, such sum to be received being prefixed by a negative sign. These sums are known as compensating variations, for if paid by the former individual, or if received by the latter individual, his welfare will remain unchanged.

Assuming n persons are affected, if the condition $\sum_{i=1}^{n} V_i > 0$ is met

– if, that is, the algebraic sum of the individual compensating variations is positive – we conclude that gainers can more than compensate losers, and the value of the excess gain over loss is the value to be

attributed to the spillover effect in question. Wherever $\sum_{i=1}^{n} V_i < 0$,

however, an excess of loss over gain is to be attributed to the spillover. There may well be cases where part, or all, of these compensatory variations are determined directly by reference to market prices. The cost of the extra laundry bills arising from industrial smoke is a popular example. Crop damage done by straying cattle is another. But, in the last resort, the value individually attributed to the spillover effect is subjective, and is to be conceived as the exact sum of money, to be paid or to be received, that restores a person's welfare to its original pre-spillover level.

Wherever the type and size of the project is given to us by technology, the question of whether or not the project should be undertaken can properly be answered only by taking into account *all* the effects arising from the construction and operation of the project; all the costs and all the benefits and, therefore, all the spillover effects also. If, for example, building a dam for irrigational purposes has the following incidental consequences: (1) it creates an artificial lake in which people can swim or boat; (2) it spoils the fishing; (3) it provides a body of stagnant water which causes a rapid increase in the insect populations in the vicinity, the first is a positive spillover, the latter two are negative spillovers. Each is to be evaluated in the manner stated above, and added together algebraically to the excess benefits (positive or negative) of the project.

2. There will be occasions, however, when the economist is presented with a number of alternative projects that differ only in size of plant and, therefore, in the volume of outputs produced. He then compares successively larger sizes of plant in order to discover the difference made to benefits and costs. Starting with some size of plant that yields excess benefits over costs, it should be obvious that so long as further increments of plant size confer more benefit than cost there is an advantage in increasing the plant size. And it goes without saying that the associated increments of spillover, positive or negative, should be added algebraically to the benefit side of the calculation. Some spillovers, however, may or may not vary with the size of the project. A small dam, for example, may destroy the fishing just as much as a large dam.

The size of these increments, in the limiting case, could be so small that for all practical purposes the changes in the plant size can be regarded as continuous. In this limiting case we are then in the familiar textbook world of continuous curves, comparing long-run marginal cost with long-run marginal benefit—except, of course, that for private goods each person's marginal benefit is coterminous with the existing demand price, whereas for collective goods the marginal benefit is the aggregate of benefits conferred simultaneously on all persons by the marginal unit of the collective good.

It is not to be supposed for a moment, however, that cost-benefit analysis confines itself to evaluating collective goods. A railroad or hospital is not, strictly speaking, a collective good; the services produced by either can be separately allocated to each of a number of persons just as a loaf of bread can be allocated to a person for his own particular consumption. And for that matter, the construction of a bakery might warrant a cost-benefit analysis, with the initial size of the plant and, later on, the output to be produced, determined on the marginal cost pricing rule.

3. In the absence of all spillovers, the necessary rule requiring marginal valuation to the community to be equal to the marginal cost of the good in question[1] is valid both for collective goods and single goods. For a single good, as distinct from a collective good, however, each person separately enjoys the amount of the good that he chooses: the consumption by person A of five loaves of bread a week is deemed to provide no satisfaction whatsoever to any one else. Thus, as distinct from a collective good, the single good has to meet a stricter condition: namely, that the amounts chosen by each person are such that the marginal valuation of bread for each one of them is exactly the same.[2] This is not, in general, true of collective goods: the last foot of width to a bridge, or the last acre to a national park, being valued differently by different people. This stricter condition for single goods is met in perfectly competitive equilibrium since each person equates his own marginal valuation to the price of the good, which price is of course equal to marginal cost.[3]

This necessary rule, stated above, and valid both for collective and single goods, has to be modified in an obvious way if, now, spillover effects accompany the production or consumption of the goods in question. Consider first a single good. If the bakery emits smoke which irritates people in the vicinity, and this irritating smoke varies directly with the number of loaves produced, smoke will be allocatively significant in determining the optimal output. The marginal valuation to society of the existing output of loaves is no longer just equal to the price that each and any of the n consumers is prepared to pay for his own marginal loaf of bread. For in order to meet the demand for any additional loaf, the bakery must emit some additional smoke. From the value to society of an additional loaf one has

[1] Although this marginal-cost rule rolls easily from the tongue, care must be exercised in its interpretation. For though each consumer equates his marginal valuation of a loaf to the market price of a loaf and, in perfect competition, therefore, to the marginal cost of a loaf, it does not follow that *each* of, say, n consumers has a marginal valuation equal to the marginal cost of producing loaves of bread. Supposing the marginal cost curve of producing loaves of bread rises smoothly, the marginal *cost* is below the marginal valuation of each of the consumers save the nth (where any of the n consumers could be the nth consumer). For the remaining $n-1$ consumers, the incremental unit cost of a loaf is, in varying degrees, below their marginal valuation of a loaf.

[2] If there is only one price for each single good on the market, then the so-called exchange optimum condition is also met: further advantageous exchange of such goods as between persons is not possible.

[3] This is a necessary though not sufficient condition for optimal output in a partial setting. It is further required (1) that total conditions be met, i.e. that there be an excess of total benefit over total cost, and (2) that there be no other output which has a greater excess benefit over cost. (If these conditions are met, 'second order' conditions need not be met.)

therefore to subtract the sum of minimal compensatory payments, $\sum_{i=1}^{n} V_i$, which sum would be necessary to restore the welfare of the n smoke victims. Prior to any correction, the competitive equilibrium output would be one where the marginal valuation of loaves alone was equal to marginal cost, but where the marginal valuation of the joint loaf-and-smoke product was below its marginal cost. In order to meet the optimal condition for this joint product, the output has to be reduced below the competitive equilibrium (so raising the marginal valuation of loaves) until the marginal *social* valuation – that of the loaf and its associated spillovers – is positive, and equal to, marginal cost. The alternative statement, that optimal output is determined at the point where the price of the good is set equal to its marginal *social* cost, is the result simply of transferring the calculated value of the associated spillovers to the other side of the equation. In this loaf example, instead of *subtracting* the calculated loss of the smoke damage from the value of the marginal loaf, the sum is *added* instead to the marginal cost of the loaf. Positive spillover effects, or, to be more precise, spillover effects that are on balance advantageous to society, are treated in the same manner, a positive sign for the compensatory sum substituting for the negative one above. Optimal output is therefore, in such cases, greater than competitive equilibrium output.

The same adjustment is required for collective goods. If some collective good, say a dam, has both positive and negative spillovers, say it provides boating but spoils the fishing, the net sums for all persons in the community are added algebraically, and the resulting total added algebraically to the marginal benefit of the collective good – or else subtracted, algebraically, from the marginal cost of the good.

4. A conscientious cost-benefit study, it is hardly necessary to remark, cannot ignore any spillover effect, positive or negative, that is of social concern. Although the value of some spillovers will be harder to estimate than others, the principle of evaluation indicated in this chapter may not be abandoned as a guide to the methods of calculation to be adopted. To adopt some other principle, such as deriving a value from the outcome of the political decision-making process, is to adopt a principle that is inconsistent with the Pareto criterion on which the estimates of the other, more measurable, items are based – on which, indeed, all allocative judgments are made in

economics. A harsher judgment of this practice would regard it as tantamount to deception. For the economist is given his brief by a political authority in order to make an estimate according to independent *economic* principles, not in order to rationalize the political process. We shall have more to say about the tendency of economists to resort occasionally to this sort of subterfuge in the next chapter on estimating the value to society of loss of life and limb.

CHAPTER 18

Evaluating Accidents and Death

1. Proper allowance in cost-benefit analysis has to be made for losses or gains arising from changes in the incidence of death, disablement or disease caused by the operation of new projects or developments.

Since the analysis of saving life is symmetrical with that of losing it, it will simplify the exposition if, initially, we confine ourselves to the analysis of *loss* of life and limb – or, more briefly, to loss of life alone – indicating the necessary extensions later on.

2. (a) Despite repeated expressions of dissatisfaction with the method, the most common way of calculating the economic worth of a person's life and, therefore, the loss to the economy consequent upon his decease, is that of discounting to the present the person's expected future earnings. This sort of calculations is occasionally supplemented by a suggestion that auxiliary calculations be made in order to take account of the suffering of the victim, his loss of utility from ceasing to be alive, and/or of the bereavement of his family.

(b) A second method, which might be thought more refined than the first, is that of calculating the present discounted value of the losses over time accruing to *others* as a result of the death of this particular individual. This method, sometimes referred to as the 'net output' approach (in order to distinguish it from the preceding method, which is referred to as the 'gross output' approach), though occasionally mentioned in the literature,[1] has not been employed apparently because of some uneasiness about the moral implications.

(c) A third possible method would repudiate any direct calculation of the loss of potential earnings or spending. Instead, it would approach the problem from a 'social' point of view. Since society, through its political processes, does in fact take decisions on investment expenditures that occasionally increase or reduce the number of deaths, an implicit value of human life can be calculated. This approach receives occasional mention[2] and, indeed, the appeal to

1 For instance, be Devons (1961, p. 107) and Ridker (1967, p. 36).
2 For instance, by Fromm (1965, p. 193) and by Schelling (1968, p. 147).

the political, or democratic, process is sometimes invoked to provide guidance on broader issues.[3]

(d) The insurance principle is a departure from any of the aforementioned methods. By making use of the premium a man is willing to pay, and the probability of his being killed as a result of engaging in some specific activity, it is thought possible to be able to calculate the value a man sets on his life.[4]

3.   Each of these four possible methods of measuring the loss of life is now briefly appraised.

Method (a), turning on the loss of potential future earnings, can be rationalized only if the criterion adopted in any economic reorganization turns on the value of its contribution to GNP, or, more accurately, to net national product. But although financial journalists manage to convey the contrary impression, maximizing GNP is not an acceptable goal of economic policy. If it were, the simplest way of promoting it would be to adopt a policy of virtually unlimited immigration – accepting immigrants up to the point at which the value of their marginal product is zero. Recourse to this method by the practising economist does not, therefore, rest on the clear recognition of the desirability of maximizing GNP but rather, obviously on the fact that it lends itself easily to quantification. Notwithstanding its usage, most writers have mental reservations about its validity, and tend to regard it as only part of the total measurement. For instance, Schelling (1968) makes a distinction between the value of livelihood and the value of life, which poses a perplexing and possibly unsolvable problem.

The so-called net output method (b) might seem, at first glance, more acceptable than the gross output method. For, taking a cold-blooded attitude, what matters to the rest of society is simply the resulting loss, or gain, to it following the death of one or more of its members. This *ex post* approach, however, appears to strike some writers as either absurd or dangerous.[5] If accepted, it certainly

---

[3]   Indeed, Rothenberg (1961, pp. 309–36) ends his examination of social welfare criteria by proposing that the democratic process itself be regarded as such a criterion. More recently, Nath (1969, pp. 216–17) proposes that the task of the economist be limited to that of revealing the locus of 'efficient' economic production possibilities available to society, leaving it to democracy to select the collection of goods it wishes.

[4]   An example is given by Fromm (1965, p. 194).

[5]   For example, Devons (1961, p. 108) concludes ironically: 'Indeed if we could only kill off enough old people we could show a net gain on accidents as a whole!' As for Ridker (1967, p. 36), the net output method 'suggests that society should not interfere with the death of a person where net value is negative'.

follows that the death of any person whose (b) measure is negative confers a net benefit on society. And this category of persons would certainly include all retired people irrespective of their ownership of property. Yet from this undeniable inference, no dread policy implications follow. If the method were satisfactory on economic grounds, the inference would not, of itself, provide any reason for rejecting it. But the method is not satisfactory for the simple reason that it has no regard to the feelings of the potential victims. It restricts itself to the interests only of the surviving members of society: it ignores society *ex ante*, and concentrates wholly on society *ex post*.

As for method (c), which would build on implicit values placed on human life by the political process, the justification appears somewhat circular even when we ignore the political realities of Western democracies: in particular (i) the fact that decisions to invest in certain projects are not determined by popular vote; instead, governments avail themselves of a general mandate, conferred on them by an election, to delegate powers of decision at various levels of the political hierarchy; (ii) the fact that investment decisions are not motivated primarily by the desire to advance the *general* welfare, on any plausible criterion, but are rather the outcome of political conflicts; and (iii) the fact that an implicit value attributable to loss of life by a particular public programme will differ widely from an implicit value derived from another public programme. Ignoring these political realities, and assuming that democratic voting alone determines whether or not a particular investment project, or part of a project, is to be adopted, the idea of deriving quantitative values from the political process is clearly contrary to the idea of deriving them from an independent economic criterion. And where the outcome of the political debate is that of calling upon the economist to provide a quantitative evaluation of the project under consideration, the economist fails to meet his brief in so far as he abandons the attempt to calculate any aspect of the project by reference to an economic criterion and instead attempts to extricate figures from previous political decisions.[6] By recourse to a method that refers a question, or part of a question, received from the political process back again to the political process, the economist appears to be concealing some deficiency in the relevant data or some weakness in the logic of his criteria. Moreover, even if it were agreed that the loss

---

[6] Which is not to deny that the economist's criterion or criteria – though independent of the outcome of any particular political process that is sanctioned by the constitution – must themselves be vindicated ultimately by reference to value judgments widely held within the community. The reader interested in this aspect is referred to my monograph (1969a, pp. 13–23).

of human life should not be estimated by 'ordinary' economic criteria used in evaluating other gains and losses, the requirements of consistency cannot be met by such implicit – and also arbitrary and erratic – valuations of political outcomes, though they might be met by particular criteria that make the valuation of loss of life explicit and systematic. As we shall see, however, there is no call for evaluating loss of life on a criterion different from that which is basic to the economist's calculation of all the other effects comprehended in a cost-benefit analysis.

Finally, there is method (d) based on the insurance principle. This has about it a superficial plausibility, enough at any rate to attract some attention. But the insurance policy makes provision, in the event of a man's death, only for compensation to *others*. Thus, the amount of insurance a man takes out may be interpreted as a reflection, *inter alia*, of his concern for his family and dependents, but hardly as an index of the value he sets on his own life. A bachelor with no dependents could have no reason to take out flight insurance, notwithstanding the fact that he could be as reluctant as the next man to depart this life at short notice.

4. The crucial objection to each of these four methods, however, is that not one of them is consistent with the basic rationale of the economic calculus used in cost-benefit analysis. If we are concerned, as we are in all allocative problems, with increasing society's satisfaction in some sense, and if in addition we eschew interpersonal comparisons of satisfactions, we can always be guided in the ranking of alternative economic arrangements by the notion of a Pareto improvement – an improvement such that at least one person is made better off and nobody is made worse off. A *potential* Parteo improvement, one where the net gains *can* so be distributed that at least one person is made better off with none being made worse off, provides an alternative criterion, or definition, of social gain – one which, as indicated earlier, provides the rationale of all familiar allocative propositions in economics, and therefore the rationale of all cost-benefit calculations.

CHAPTER 19

Evaluating Accidents and Death (continued)

1.   Consistency with the criterion of a potential Pareto improvement and, therefore, consistency with the principle of evaluation in cost-benefit analyses, would require that the loss of a person's life be valued with reference to his compensating variations; with reference, that is, to the minimum sum he is prepared to accept in exchange for its surrender. For unless a project that is held to be responsible for, say, an additional one thousand deaths annually can show an excess of benefits over costs *after* meeting the compensatory sums necessary to restore the welfare of these one thousand victims, it is not possible to make all members of the community better off by a redistribution of the net gains. A potential Pareto improvement cannot then be achieved, and the project in question ought not to be admitted.

If the argument is accepted, however, the requirements of consistency might seem to be highly restrictive. Since an increase in the annual number of deaths can be confidently predicted in connection with a number of particular developments – those, for example, which contribute to an increase in ground and air traffic – such developments would no longer appear as economically feasible. For it would not surprise us to discover that, in ordinary circumstances, no sum of money is large enough to compensate a man for the loss of his life.

2.   In conditions of certainty, the logic of the above proposition is unassailable. If in ordinary circumstances we face a person with the choice of continuing his life in the usual way, or of ending it at noon on the morrow, a finite sum large enough to persuade him to choose the latter course of action may not exist. And indeed if the development in question unavoidably entailed the death of this specific person or, more generally, a number of specific persons, it is highly unlikely that any conceivable excess benefit over cost (calculated in the absence of these fatalities) would warrant its undertaking on the potential Pareto criterion.

It is never the case, however, that a specific person, or a number of specific persons, can be designated in advance as being those who are certain to be killed if a particular project is undertaken.[1] All that can

---

[1]   Cf. Schelling's remarks (1968, pp. 142–6).

be predicted, though with a high degree of confidence, is that out of a total of n members in the community, an additional x members per annum will be killed (and, say, an additional $10x$ members will be seriously injured). In the absence, therefore, of any breakdown of the circumstances surrounding the additional number of accidents to be expected, the increment of risk of being killed imposed each year on any one member of the community can be taken as x/n (and $10x/n$ for the risk of being seriously injured). And it is this fact of complete ignorance of the identity of each of the potential victims that transforms the calculation. Assuming universal risk aversion,[2] the relevant sums to be subtracted from the benefit side are no longer those which compensate a *specific* number of persons for their certain death, but are those which compensate each person in the community for the additional risk to which he is to be exposed.

In general, of course, every activity will have attached to it some discernible degree of risk (even staying at home in bed bears some risk of mishap – the bed might collapse; the wind might blow the roof in; a marauder might enter). Any change, from one environment to another, from one style of living to another, can be said to alter the balance of risk, sometimes imperceptibly, sometimes substantially. Only the dead opt out of all risk. Yet the actual statistical risk attaching to some activity may be so small that only the hypersensitive would take account of it. In common with all other changes in economic arrangements, there is some *minimum sensible* beyond which an increment, or decrement, of risk will go unnoticed. More important, however, what is strictly relevant to the analysis is not the change in the statistical risk *per se*, but the person's response, if any, to such a change. For the change in risk may go unperceived and, if perceived, it may be improperly evaluated. Indeed, people do have difficulty in grasping the objective significance of large numbers and, where chance or risk is at issue, they are prone to underestimate it. One chance in 50,000 of winning a lottery, or of having one's house burned down, seems a better chance, or a greater risk, than it actually is. And if so, the existence of gambling and insurance by the same person is explicable without recourse to the ingenious Friedman-Savage hypothesis (1948).

The analysis, however, does not depend upon the veracity of such

[2] Risk-aversion is assumed throughout (unless otherwise stated) solely in the interests of brevity. If some people enjoy the additional risk, their CVs will be positive. In general if the aggregate of the CVs for the additional risk is negative, which is the case for universal risk aversion, there is a subtraction from the benefit side. If, on the other hand, it were positive, there would be an addition to the benefit side.

conjectures. All the reader has to accept is the proposition that it is peoples' subjective preferences of the worth of a thing that counts. In the market place, the price of a good, or a 'bad' (such as labour-input or other disutility), is fixed by the producer, and the buyer or seller determines the amount by reference to his subjective preferences. Where, however, the amount of a (collective) good, or 'bad', is fixed for each person – as may be the case with a change in risk – a person's subjective preference can only determine the price he will accept or offer for it. Peoples' imperfect knowledge of economic opportunities, their imprudence and unworldliness, has never prevented economists from accepting as basic data the amounts people freely choose at given prices. Such imperfections cannot therefore consistently be invoked to qualify people's choices when, instead, their preferences are exercised in placing a price on some increment of a good or 'bad'. True, attempts to observe the change of magnitude when people adjust the price to the change in quantity – rather than the more common assumption that they adjust the quantity to the change in price – does pose problems of measurement. But the problems of measurement must not be allowed to obscure the validity of the concept.[3]

Placed within their broadest possible context, then, any additional risk of death, associated with the provision of some new facility, takes its place as one of a number of economic consequences (including employment gains and losses, new purchase and sale opportunities, and the withdrawal of existing ones) all of which affect the welfare of each of the n members of the community.

3. A word on the deficiencies in the information available to each person concerning the degree of risk involved. These deficiencies of information necessarily contribute to the discrepancies experienced by people between anticipated and realized satisfaction. For all that, in determining whether a potential Pareto improvement has been met, economists are generally agreed – either as a canon of faith, as a political tenet, or as an act of expediency – to accept the dictum

[3] It has been put to me by a colleague that 'the benefits of increased safety from a project can be worth no more than the cost of preserving human life (or of a reduction in accidents) by alternative means'. This statement, however, confuses the measure of the benefits themselves with the measure of the expenditures necessary to produce such benefits. The economist must obviously consider 'alternative means' in order to produce any good at its lowest cost. But he cannot know whether incurring the lowest possible cost is justified until he has independently calculated a figure for the benefits in question, so enabling him to estimate the excess social benefit, or social loss, of preserving human life etc.

that each person knows his own interest best. If, therefore, the economist is told that a person A is indifferent as between not assuming a particular risk and assuming it along with a sum of money, V, then, on the Pareto principle, the sum V has to be accepted as the relevant cost of his being exposed to that risk. It may well be the case that, owing either to deficient information, or congenital optimism, person A consistently overestimates his chances of survival. But once the dictum is accepted, as indeed it is in economists' appraisals of allocative efficiency, cost-benefit analysis has to accept V as the only relevant magnitude – this being the sum chosen by A in awareness of his relative ignorance.[4] Certainly all the rest of the economic data used in a cost-benefit analysis, or any other allocative study, whether derived from market prices and quantities, or by other methods of enquiry, is based on this principle of accepting as final only the individual's estimate of what a thing is worth to him at the time the decision is to be made. The thing in question may, of course, also have a direct worth, positive or negative, for persons other than the buyer or seller of it, a possibility which requires a consideration of external effects. Yet, again, on the above dictum, it is the values placed on this thing by these other persons that are to count. Thus, while it is scarcely necessary to urge that more economical ways of refining and disseminating information be explored, the economist engaged in allocative studies traditionally follows the practice of evaluating all social gains and losses solely on the basis of individuals' own evaluations of the relevant effects on their welfare, given the information they have at the time the decision is taken.

Person A, for example, may find himself disabled for life and rue his decision to take the risk. But this example is only a more painful reminder of the fact that people come to regret a great many of the choices they make, notwithstanding which they would resent any interference with their future choices.

CHAPTER 20

In Conclusion

In our growth-fevered atmosphere there is always a strong temptation for the economist, as for other specialists, to come up with firm quantitative results. In order to be able to do so, however, he finds that he must ignore the less easily measured spillovers. In so far as the ignored spillover effects are adverse, this common response to the temptation imparts a bias toward favouring commercially viable projects, irrespective of their ability to withstand more searching criteria. As a matter of professional pride, and of obligation to the community he elects to serve, the economist should resist this temptation.

Yet, it may well be asked, until such time as more reliable methods are evolved to bring these spillovers into the calculus, what can the economist do? The least he can do is to reveal clearly the area of ignorance. After measuring all that can be measured with honesty, he can provide a physical description of the spillovers and some idea of their significance. Secondly, he may offer a guess, or a range of guesses, about the value of damage to be expected. He will certainly avoid spurious quantification – spurious because based on invalid concepts. Thirdly, and as a development of the preceding suggestion, he can have recourse to what I have called elsewhere (1969a) *contingency calculations*, these being the hypothetical estimates of a critical magnitude for the spillovers which are just large enough to offset the excess benefits of a project that are calculated in disregard of the spillovers.

To illustrate, if the cost-benefit calculation of a new airport produces an excess benefit over cost of some $10 millions per annum for the next t years, but only by ignoring the aircraft noise it generates, the increased traffic congestion it causes, and the increased loss of life that is expected to follow, the economist can impress the authorities, and the public with the importance of these consequences by making hypothetical estimates of a critical *average* loss per person, or per family, based on rough calculations of the numbers of people likely to be affected. Thus (a), if it were reckoned that about half a million additional families would suffer in varying degrees as a result of the newly-located airport, an annual compensatory sum averaging as little as $20 per family would wholly offset the excess benefit. Again (b), if the new airport becomes responsible for adding to the road congestion within the region of the airport, so as to cause an average delay of one hour a week to about one million motorists, this delay alone if valued at 20 cents an hour, would wholly offset the $10 million of excess benefits of the project. Similarly for loss of life, and any other remaining side effects.

Even though the estimate of the number of people affected is speculative, provided it is not altogether implausible, the resulting contingency calculations may well cast doubt on the economic feasibility of the scheme – enough doubt, at least, to delay a decision until estimates of these less tangible, but socially important, features of the scheme can be made with greater assurance. On the other hand, there may be instances in which the per person, or per family, valuation of the spillover deriving from the contingency calculation will be so large as to place the economic feasibility of the scheme beyond doubt.

Finally, there is nothing to prevent the economist from using the questionnaire method to secure information that is not thrown up, directly or indirectly, by the pricing system. True, economists have tended to scorn this source of data, and their scorn may be forgiven wherever more dependable information is to be had by observing what a man does rather than listening to what he says of himself. In particular, where behavioural relations are at issue, as they are in 'positive economics', there is everything to be said for this conservative practice: if the evidence does not suffice, we can always wait.

But when it comes to evaluating spillover effects in a cost-benefit analysis, one cannot wait for more 'objective' information. Without some market mechanism by which people can express their attitudes to spillover effects, there can be no 'objective' way of measuring their costs. Indeed, the description of the nature of adverse environmental spillover effects, as unavoidable *collective* bads, itself suggests that the likelihood of a market mechanism being established for such effects is remote. Surveys based on the questionnaire method may be suspect for a number of reasons, but they are sometimes better than guesswork, and assuredly better than no information at all. The economist in earnest about making cost-benefit analysis a more discriminating technique will be giving plenty of thought to the measurement of environmental spillovers and, in consequence, plenty of thought also to the possibilities of evolving questionnaire techniques for eliciting critical information.[1]

[1] No matter how fastidious the recommendation of the economist, it cannot be depended upon to secure majority approval. The economic policies adopted by majorities will generally be less than ideal. Such losses arising from existing political mechanisms have not been treated in these chapters. The reader interested in such problems should find stimulating reading in Buchanan and Tullock's *Calculus of Consent*.

References and Bibliography for Part III

Buchanan, J. M., 'An Economic Theory of Clubs', *Economica*, 1965.
———— and Stubblebine, W. C., 'Externality', *Economica*, 1962.
———— and Tullock, G., *The Calculus of Consent*, Michigan: University of Michigan Press, 1962.
Burrows, P., 'Nuisance: The Law and Economics', *Lloyd's Bank Review*, 1970.
———— 'On External Cost & The Visible Arm of The Law', *Oxford Econ. Papers*, 1970.
Coase, H., 'The Problems of Social Cost', *Journal of Law and Economics*, 1960.
Devons, E., *Essays in Economics*, London: Allen & Unwin, 1961.
Dobb, M., *Welfare Economics and the Economics of Socialism*, Cambridge: Cambridge University Press, 1969.
Fromm, G., 'Civil Aviation Expenditures', in R. Dorfman (ed.), *Measuring Benefits of Government Investment*, Washington D.C.: Brookings Institution, 1965 (London: Allen & Unwin, 1968).
———— Comment on T. C. Schelling's paper, 'The Life You Save May Be Your Own', in S. B. Chase, Jr. (ed.), *Problems in Public Expenditure*, Washington D.C.: Brookings Institution, 1968 (London: Allen & Unwin, 1968).
Graaff, J. de V., *Theoretical Welfare Economics*, Cambridge: Cambridge University Press, 1957.
Kneese, A. V., 'Research Goals and Progress Toward Them', in H. Jarrett (ed.), *Environmental Quality in a Growing Economy*, London: John Hopkins Press, 1967.
Marshall, A., *Principles of Economics* (8th edn), London: Macmillan, 1925.
McKean, R., *Efficiency in Government Through Systems Analysis with Emphasis on Water Resource Development*, London: Wiley, 1958.
Misham, E. J., 'A Reappraisal of the Principles of Resource Allocation', *Economica*, 1957.
———— 'Rent as a Measure of Welfare Change', *American Economic Review*, 1959.
———— *Welfare Economics: An Assessment*, Amsterdam: North Holland Publishing Company, 1969(a).
———— 'The Relationship between Joint Products, Collective Goods, and External Effects', *Journal of Political Economy*, 1969(b).
———— 'The Postwar Literature on Externalities: An Interpretive Essay', *Journal of Economic Literature*, March 1971.
Nath, S. K., *A Reappraisal of Welfare Economics*, London: Routledte & Kegan Paul, 1969.
Oort, C. J., *Decreasing Costs as a Problem of Welfare Economics*, Amsterdam, 1958.
Pigou, A. C., *Economics of Welfare* (4th ed.), London: Macmillan, 1946.
Reynolds, D. J., 'The Cost of Road Accidents', *Journal of the Royal Statistical Society*, 1956.
Ridker, R. G., *The Economic Costs of Air Pollution*, New York: F. A. Praeger, 1967.
Schelling, T. C., 'The Life You Save May Be Your Own', in S. B. Chase, Jr. (ed.), *Problems in Public Expenditure*, Washington, D.C.; Brookings Institution, 1968 (London: Allen & Unwin, 1968).
Turvey, R., 'On Divergencies between Social Cost and Private Cost', *Economica*, 1963.

CHAPTER 21

Introduction

1. The benefits from an investment project come to fruition over the future. Some of the costs incurred by undertaking the investment may also take place over the future. In general, then, there is a distinct time-profile of benefits and costs corresponding to each of the investment projects under consideration. Since we are concerned with *social* benefits and not business profits net of taxes, any part of the gross revenues, or calculated benefits, that are used in paying income taxes or corporation taxes are *not* to be subtracted from such revenues or benefits. Nor for that matter are excise taxes to be subtracted from the market price of the goods produced by the project in calculating the social value of the outputs. All such taxes are to be regarded as transfers of value from the enterprise and its consumers to the public at large.

The continuous flow of future benefits and costs is in practice broken up into discrete magnitudes. For example, B_0, B_1, B_2, ... B_n, could stand successively for the total benefits expected during year zero (the current year; that is the year during which the investment is undertaken); the total benefits expected during the next year, year one; the total benefits expected during year two, and so on to the total benefits expected in the final, or n^{th}, year. Similarly, the profile of costs over time can be represented by K_0, K_1, K_2, ..., K_n, where K_0 stands for the expected initial outlay; K_1 the expected total outlay in the following year, year one; K_2 the expected total outlay in year two, and so on until the final total outlay in the nth year. The stream of *net* benefits, or *excess* benefits over costs, can therefore be written as $(B_0 - K_0)$, $(B_1 - K_1)$, $(B_2 - K_2)$, ..., $(B_n - K_n)$, in which total benefits are to be understood in the most comprehensive sense to include all additions to social welfare, and total costs or outlays are to include all resource costs reckoned as opportunity costs.[1] It

[1] These total outlays are usually restricted to *capital* costs and total benefits to net (potential) revenues. Current operation costs, which include factor payments and payments for raw materials and intermediate goods, are therefore conventionally excluded from the magnitude of the outlays. This convention does not always hold, however, and such costs can be included (along with any interest payments to the banks for use of a 'revolving fund' in order to meet regular outgoings) provided that the benefits then are calculated as the value of sales during any year, along with any increase or decrease of inventories.

112

goes without saying that – excluding the initial and the nth net benefit – some of the net benefits may be zero, the remainder being positive or negative. However, it is often the case that all the capital outlays will be incurred during the first year, or during the first one or two years, after which there will be a succession of net benefits.

The question we are to ask is, how should we rank a number of alternative investment streams of this sort, and, indeed, should we undertake any of them?

2. To take a simplified example of four investment opportunities, A_1, A_2, A_3, and A_4, having net benefits shown in Table IV.1 below:

Table IV.1

	1	2	3	4	5
A_1	−100	115	0	0	0
A_2	−100	20	30	50	170
A_3	−100	100	110	−50	0
A_4	−100	80	110	−50	−10

If we had to choose *only one* from the four, we could be sure that it would never be A_4, irrespective of the criterion used. For A_3 is as good as, or better than, A_4 period for period. In the jargon, investment option A_3 'dominates' A_4. Thus, if we subtract A_4's net benefit stream from that of A_3 the difference is a series, 0, 20, 10, 0, 10, these figures showing the amount by which A_3's net benefits exceed those of A_4 in successive periods. In no period is A_3's net benefit less than that of A_4.[2]

Let us now consider four rather crude investment criteria which, however, are commonly employed in the business sector, expecially where the venture contemplated is risky.

(a) *Cut-off period.* This is perhaps the crudest possible criterion that is used in business in order to decide whether or not to invest in a project. A period is chosen over which the money invested must be fully recouped. The period could be ten years, though usually a shorter period such as five years, or even less, is chosen. Such a criterion may be justified in cases of innovation in products, or methods, that cannot be protected by patent, and which innovations

[2] If, on the other hand, we had funds enabling us to choose two or more of these investment options, we might choose both A_3 and A_4. But we should never include A_4 while rejecting A_3.

113

are likely to be copied by competing firms within two or three years. A cut-off period of three years, for instance, may be chosen in the belief that after three years further profits are uncertain, and increasingly unlikely. Glancing down the Table, it is clear that a cut-off period of three years *after* the initial outlay would admit the A_1 investment option. Indeed, more than the initial 100 is recouped in the first year after the outlay. The A_2 option only just scrapes home. A_3 would be able to recoup as much as 160 in the three years, while A_4 would recoup 130 (which, however, would be 120 if the *outlay* of 10 in the fourth year were certain).

The shortcomings of this criterion are easy to perceive. If the returns were not expected to accrue mainly in the first few years but mainly after the first few years, worthwhile projects would be rejected. A stream – 100, 0, 0, 20, 40, 60, 80, 120, . . . would be rejected. So also would a stream – 100, 20, 20, 20, 20, 20, 20, . . .

(b) *Pay-off period.* Instead of choosing an arbitrary cut-off period, we may rank the investment options according to the number of years necessary to recoup the initial outlay. Clearly the A_1 project would be ranked first, since its pay-off period is less than a year. For the A_2 project it is exactly three years. For the last two investment projects it is two years—even after subtracting the later outlays.

The so-called *pay-off period rate of return* is but another way of expressing the same results. It is obtained simply by dividing 100 by the number of years in the pay-off period. If the A_1 investment option requires only a year to pay off the initial outlay, it is equal to 100 per cent (actually it is a bit more than 100 per cent as the outlay of 100 is paid off in less than a year). For the A_2 project, the pay-off period rate of return is equal to 100 divided by 3, or $33\frac{1}{3}$ per cent. For the other two investment options it is about 50 per cent.

The justification for either form of this ranking device is similar to that for the cut-off period. When imitation by competitors, or rapid obsolescence is anticipated, or in circumstances of political uncertainty, one of the overriding considerations is safety. One looks for quick returns and prepares for a hasty exit. A project such as A_1, which pays 115 within a year of 100 being invested is likely, in such circumstances, to be looked on with greater favour than option A_2 which would not show any profit until the fourth year.

In the complete absence of uncertainty, however, it would be impossible to justify either of the above rules-of-thumb. If interest rates happened to be low, A_2 would be far more profitable than A_1, and more profitable than A_3 for that matter.

(c) *Average rate of return.* This is the simplest way of taking account of all the figures in the investment stream. Just because all the figures

114

are taken at face value in calculating the average rate of return, there is an implied assumption that all the figures have been corrected for uncertainty.

For all investment options having only the initial outlay of 100, such as A_1 and A_2 in Table IV.1, there is no ambiguity in the method. One simply adds together all the subsequent positive net benefits, divides this sum by the number of years, and expresses the resulting figure as a percentage of the initial investment outlay. For the A_1 option, the sum of positive benefits is 115. This sum divided by one gives an average sum of 115 per annum, and expressed as a percentage of the outlay of 100, is 115 per cent. For A_2 the sum over four years of the positive benefits is 270. This sum divided by 4 gives an annual average return of $67\frac{1}{2}$ and, expressed as a percentage of the original outlay of 100, is $67\frac{1}{2}$ per cent.

The weakness of this method is apparent at once. For it is by no means evident to anyone thinking of investing 100 that A_1, with an average rate of return of 115 per cent, is superior to A_2. It might be added in passing, however, that the weakness is not particular to this method, but also arises in the more sophisticated internal-rate-of-return method which will be treated later.

For investment options A_3 and A_4, having outlays in later years, the method has not been specified. On the one hand, we could add together all the figures, both positive and negative, after the initial outlay and proceed as before. For A_3 the algebraic sum of 100, 110, and -50, is 160. This sum divided by 3 yields an average of $53\frac{1}{3}$ per cent per annum. Similarly for A_4 which yields an average return of $32\frac{1}{2}$ per cent. Alternatively, we could total the outlays first, work out the average amount of the remaining positive figures (210 for A_3, 190 for A_4), and divide by the number of years yielding a positive investment. This sum is then taken as a percentage of the sum of the outlays (150 for A_3, 160 for A_4). Using this method the average yield for A_3 is 70 per cent, and for A_2 is 56 per cent.

(d) *Net average rate of return* The above results can be regarded as 'gross' average yields since they are derived from adding together only the positive net benefit figures. One obvious modification is to calculate a 'net' average yield in the same way, except that the outlays are subtracted from the sum of the benefits before dividing by the number of years. In A_1, for example, we should first subtract the outlay of 100 from the 115, to give 15, this being 15 per cent of the 100 outlay. In A_2 we subtract the outlay of 100 from the positive sum of benefits, 270, before dividing by 4. Hence a net average rate of return of $42\frac{1}{2}$ per cent. The comparison between A_1 and A_2 looks a lot more plausible on this 'net' average method than on the 'gross' average method above. Again, we can treat A_3 and A_4 in the two alternative ways indicated above. The first way gives 20 per cent for A_3 and 15 per cent for A_4. The second gives 20 per cent for A_3 and 9 per cent for $\bar{A}_4$.

Under conditions of certainty, at least, the net average rate of return, though clearly superior to the other investment rules, is unsatisfactory for two reasons.

(1) It depends upon the number of years chosen. To choose the length of the investment stream by reference to the number of consecutive years showing a positive net benefit is arbitrary. For example if project A_1 in Table IV.1 yielded the slightest positive net benefit in year two – say, a return of 0.1 – the average rate of return would result from dividing the total benefits, $115 + 0.1$, *less* the initial outlay of 100, by 2 instead of one, giving 7.51, which on this method has to be accepted as the net average rate of return per annum on the 100 investment. This slight addition to the net benefit of the A_1 investment option makes it look, on this calculation, a very much less attractive proposition, a paradoxical result which could obviously cause a lot of trouble.

(2) A less apparent but no less serious defect is that the method takes no cognizance of the *pattern* or *profiile* of the net benefits over time. Given the total amount of the net benefits, say 300, arising over a number of consecutive years, whether the net benefits are bunched together over the first years, spread evenly over the years, or bunched toward the end of the period, makes not the slightest difference to the net average rate of return. An investment stream of -100, 5, 20, 25, 250 is to be valued as highly as one of -100, 250, 25, 20, 5; or, for that matter, we should on this calculation be indifferent as between an investment option having the stream -100, 1, 1, 1, 297, and one having the stream -100, 297, 1, 1, 1. But which person would not prefer the latter to the former? For people do take notice of the timing of benefits, that is they are not perfectly indifferent as between receiving $10,000 in ten years time and receiving $10,000 today. Once we take into account the time dimension, we are impelled to move away from these rather primitive investment criteria to those more familiar to economists.

3.   These more sophisticated investment criteria are all based on the common procedure of reducing a stream of net benefits (some negative, some positive) to a single value at a point of time. This is done by using some rate of interest as a weighting device through time. The more familiar fall into two categories: (1) those which

determined the *value* of an investment stream at an arbitrary point of time by reference to a given rate of interest—the more popular procedure being that of determining a *present* value of the investment stream; (2) those which determine an average *rate of return* by reference to the condition that the present value of the entire stream, when discounted by this average rate of return, reduces to zero. The more popular criterion in this connection is that known as the internal rate of return.

These two popular investment criteria, the present discounted value criterion and the internal rate of return criterion, will be compared in the following chapter.

CHAPTER 22

Discounted Present Value and Internal Rate of Returns

1. Consider first the Discounted Present Value (DPV) criterion. If we have an investment stream, $-100, 50, 150$, and we are given a rate of interest of 10 per cent per annum by which to discount it, the DPV of the stream of *benefits*[1] alone (50 in year one, 150 in year two) is calculated as follows:

$$\frac{50}{(1 + 0.1)} + \frac{150}{(1 + 0.1)} 2 = 166.5.$$

Thus, at a 10 per cent discount rate, the benefit of 50 occurring one year from the initial investment has a value at this initial, or zero, period of 50 less 10 per cent, or 45. The benefit of 150, occurring two years from the initial period, has a value of 150 less 10 per cent, or 135, in the *preceding* year, year one, and this 135 is then reduced by 10 per cent to obtain its value, 121.5, in the initial, or zero, period. The value of these two benefits, discounted to the initial, or zero, period, 45 and 121.5, are then added to give 166.5. If there were three, four, or more years of benefits, the total benefit in each year is discounted back to period zero in the same manner. These discounted benefits are then added together to give the DPV of all the benefits.

The DPV of the outlay of 100 is, of course, 100, since it is supposed to be incurred right at the beginning of the period; that is, at the beginning of the first year or, for the sake of conformity, at the end of the zero[th] year. Being incurred just at the point of time to which all subsequent benefits – and all subsequent outlays, if there are any – are to be reduced, it obviously does not require discounting to that point of time.

The *net* DPV of the above investment stream, being the DPV of the benefits *less* the DPV of the costs, is (166.5 – 100) or 66.5. If we wish to regard outlays as negative benefits, the net discounted present

---

[1] Although it is necessary to make clear to the reader that the algebraic total in any ith year $(B_t - K_t)$ is in general a *net* figure, we shall now find it convenient to change our terminology, and refer to a *net* benefit, or *excess* benefit in the ith year – that is, $(B_t - K_t)$ positive – simply as a benefit. Similarly, we shall henceforth refer to a *net* cost, or *excess* cost over benefit, in any year, simply as a cost

value of an investment stream is simply the sum of all the benefits when discounted to their present value.

In more general terms, given a stream of benefits, $B_0, B_1, B_2, \ldots,$ B_n, where the Bs are positive, zero, or negative, the net present discounted value is given by

$$B_0 + \frac{B_1}{(1+r)} + \frac{B_2}{(1+r)}2 + \ldots + \frac{B_n}{(1+r)}n,$$

or, more briefly,

$$\sum_{t=0}^{t=n} \frac{B_t}{(1+r)}t,$$

where r is the rate of discount.

The necessary instrument in this criterion is the appropriate rate of interest, or rate of discount, by which the benefit at any point of time is weighted. It is commonly assumed that the correct rate of interest is that which reflects society's rate of time preference. (If, for example, society is taken to be indifferent between having $100 million today and $106 million next year, the *social* rate of time preference is 6 per cent per annum.) We shall, for the present, go along with this assumption though later on it will be argued that it is correct only under special conditions. In a Crusoe economy, if 120 bushels of corn next year are deemed by Crusoe to be equivalent in satisfaction to 100 bushels of corn today – by which is meant that he is perfectly indifferent to having either an extra 100 bushels of corn today or 120 bushels of corn in a year's time – Crusoe's rate of discount is 20 per cent per annum. Until Man Friday arrives, and has some say in the decision, Crusoe's individual rate of discount can also be thought of as the social rate of discount.

2. To be more accurate, however, Crusoe's reaction to the choice presented to him gives us no more than the social rate of discount for the one year and, for that matter, is strictly valid only for 100 bushels of corn this year, not for more or for less. If, indeed, the same rate of discount did hold for successive years, then Crusoe would be indifferent as between 100 today, 120 next year, 144 in the year following that, and so on. It is however, quite possible that his discount rate rises with the passage of time. Instead of being indifferent as between 100 today and 144 in two years time, he might specify 150 in two years time. This would mean that for the first year his rate of discount is 20 per cent, but for the second year he uses a discount rate of roughly 25 per cent per annum.

Again, even if we confine ourselves to the one year, it is not true that the same rate of discount holds for *any* amount of corn. If Crusoe agrees, though only just, to postpone consumption of 100 bushels of corn this year in order to have an additional 120 bushels next year, it does not follow that he will be prepared to forgo another 100 bushels of corn this year in exchange for another additional 120 bushels next year. It is more plausible to suppose that he should want more than an additional 120 bushels next year to persuade him to forgo this year the consumption of yet another 100 bushels; say an additional 140 bushels next year. We could say that Crusoe's marginal willingness to sacrifice 100 today for 120 next year reflects a discount rate of 20 per cent per annum, while his marginal willingness to sacrifice 200 today for 260 tomorrow reflects a discount rate of 30 per cent over-all. Put otherwise, we could say that for the first 100 bushels the marginal discount rate was 20 per cent, and that the marginal discount rate for another 100 bushels was 40 per cent.

These possibilities are to be noted before passing on. For it is also the case in society at large that, however the social rate of discount is determined, it is invariant neither with respect to the magnitude of the intertemporal exchange of goods nor to the length of time involved. If we have information about the variation of the rate of discount with respect either to magnitude or time, however, there is no difficulty, in principle, in adapting our chosen investment criterion accordingly. In the meantime, our task will be simplified by assuming but a single social rate of discount. Moreover, since we are to examine this concept later on, we shall also assume that this social rate of discount is known to us. If the reader prefers, he can suppose, provisionally, that it has arisen from the interplay of market forces plus, perhaps, some form of government intervention that has the object of ensuring that the resulting rate of interest in the economy correctly reveals society's preference as between present and future goods. If, for instance, the social rate of discount is 10 per cent per annum, we shall take it that society as a whole is indifferent as between 100 today, 110 in a year's time, 121 in two years time, and so on. And that, therefore, the *present* value of 110 in one year's time, or 121 in two years time, is exactly 100.

3. Having made these provisional simplifications, let us go on to consider the following two propositions, each of them commonplace in the literature on the subject.

(a) The Net Present Discounted Value of a particular investment stream depends upon the rate of discount used. If, for instance, the stream of benefits is −100, 0, 150, the net present value of the stream[2] would be a little less than 48 if the discount rate were 1 per cent. If, instead, the discount rate were 50 per cent, the net present value would be −33⅓.

(b) Which of a number of investment streams yields the largest net discounted present value depends, in general, upon the rate of discount used. If the two investment streams are, respectively, −50, 20, 80, and −60, 20, 70, then the first, being dominant, will have a larger net present value irrespective of the rate of discount employed. If, instead, the two streams are, respectively, −100, 0, 180 and −100, 165, 0, a discount rate of 1 per cent ranks the first, with a net present value of about 76, above the second, which has a net present value of about 63. If, however, the rate of discount is 50 per cent, the net present value of the first stream is −20 and is, therefore, ranked *below* the second stream, which has a net present value of 10. From these two examples it should be manifest that there is a particular social rate of discount – between 1 per cent and 50 per cent – for which the two streams have exactly the same present value. Let us call this social rate of discount r^*. Then r^* is easily determined by equating the net present value formulae for the two streams, i.e. we set

$$-100 + \frac{180}{(1 + r)}\,2 = -100 + \frac{165}{(1 + r)},$$

and solve for r^*, which turns out to be about 9 per cent.

In general we can determine a net present value of a particular investment stream, say A, for each conceivable rate of discount. The resulting relationship can be plotted in Figure IV.1 where the vertical axis measures PVr, or net present value of the investment stream in question, and the horizontal axis measures r, the social rate of discount. The net present value of the A stream becomes smaller the larger is the rate of discount r; hence the negative slope of the A curve. It will be noted that the negative slope crosses the horizontal axis and continues below it into the south-east quadrant. This indicates that at discount rates above some critical rate of discount the net present value of the stream becomes negative (for example, at a 50 per cent discount rate, the stream −100, 0, 180, has a net present value of −20). A similar relationship can be plotted for a different investment stream B.

If one of these two investment streams were dominant, it would lie

<hr />

[2] The Net Present Discounted Value or, alternatively, the excess of benefits over costs (when both are discounted to the present), can be abbreviated to Net Present Value.

above the other at all rates of discount. In the absence of dominance the A and B curves will intersect, either in the positive quadrant, as in the Figure, or else in the negative quadrant (not shown). For all conceivable (positive) discount rates – save one, r^* – the present value of the two streams differs. At discount rates below r^* the A stream has a higher net discounted present value than the B stream,

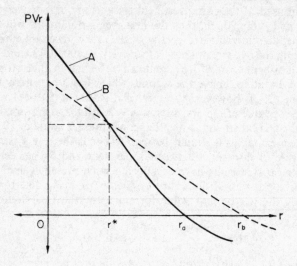

Fig IV.1

the reverse being true for discount rates above r^*. Only at r^* do both streams have the same net present value. It is obvious that if the rate of discount, from being a little above r^*, fell to a figure below r^*, the net present value of the A stream would change from being less than that of the B stream to being greater than it.

It may be observed finally, that there are two discount rates, r_a and r_b respectively, corresponding to each investment stream A and B, for which the net discounted present value of each stream is zero.

4.   Let us now turn to the internal rate of return, which is really a more respectable form of the average rate of return mentioned in the preceding chapter—more respectable in that, like the discounted present value method, it takes time into account.

A simple example will illustrate how the internal rate of return is calculated. If we have a stream of net benefits, $-100, 50, 86.4$, we can discount each of these net benefits to the present, $t = 0$, using a discount rate of 20 per cent. The present value of the benefit of 50 in year one, when discounted at 20 per cent, is $50/(1 + 0.2)$, or 40, while the present value of 86.4 in year 2, when discounted at 20 per cent, is $86.4/(1 + 0.2)^2$, or 60. The present value of both 50 in year one and 86.4 in year two is, therefore, $40 + 60$, or 100; which is exactly equal to the initial *negative* benefit, or outlay, of 100. Just because this 20 per cent discount equates the present value of the positive benefits to the present value of the outlay, it is taken to be the internal rate of return of the above stream of benefits.

The internal rate of return is, then, the rate of discount which makes the present value of the benefits exactly equal to the present value of the costs. Put otherwise, the internal rate of return is that rate of discount which makes the present value of the entire stream – benefits and costs – exactly equal to zero. Thus, if we have an investment stream,

$$B_0, B_1, B_2, \ldots, B_n, (B_i \geqslant 0, \text{ for } i = 0, 1, 2, \ldots, n),$$

then the internal rate of return λ, is that for which the sum

$$\frac{B_0}{(1 + \lambda)}0 + \frac{B_1}{(1 + \lambda)}1 + \frac{B_2}{(1 + \lambda)}2 + \ldots + \frac{B_n}{(1 + \lambda)}n = 0,$$

or, more briefly, that for which

$$\sum_{t=0}^{n} \frac{B_t}{(1 + \lambda)}t = 0.$$

The sense in which the internal rate of return, so defined, is an average over time is conveyed by the example of a man investing, say, 100 for five years. If the internal rate of return were 25 per cent per annum, the man would have in mind an equivalent, though simpler, investment in which his 100 in the present grows by 25 per cent each year. He sees his 100 in the present becoming 125 by the end of the first year, $156\frac{1}{4}$ by the end of the second year, and so on, to reach $100 (1 + 0.25)^5$ by the end of the fifth year. More generally, if the investment stream in question were $-100, B_1, B_2, B_3, B_4$, and B_5, where the Bs are any pattern of benefits, and the internal rate of return of that stream were known to be 25 per cent, then an *equivalent* investment stream would be $-100, 0, 0, 0, 0, 100 (1 + 0.25)^5$. For this latter investment stream, when discounted to its present value at 25 per cent is, by assumption, equal to zero, and so also is the equivalent stream. Consequently, if a man is told that the internal rate of an investment stream over n years is equal to λ, he is justified in thinking of the investment as equivalent to one in which his initial outlay is compounded forward at the rate of λ per annum for n years.

Thinking of the internal rate of return in this way, the man will want to compare any such investment with the opportunities for putting his money into other securities, either equities or government bonds. If the only alternative open to him, or the only alternative he will consider, is long-term government bonds, perpetuities say, yielding 6 per cent per annum,[3] then an investment yielding an internal rate of return of more than 6 per cent (always assuming certainty or, at least, equal certainty) will be preferred to the purchase of these 6 per cent government bonds.

Returning now to *public* investment criteria, the correct internal rate of return corresponding to each of the projects being contemplated can be directly compared one with the other and ranked accordingly. Each can also be compared with the alternative internal rate of return from leaving the outlay in the private sector. In the event that the outlay of 100 is raised entirely by reducing consumption, this opportunity forgone has an internal rate of time exactly equal to r, society's rate of time preference. For at this rate r, society is indifferent between 100 in the initial year and $100 (1+r)$ in the following year and $100 (1+r)^n$ in the nth year. If, therefore, consumption of 100 is deferred in year zero, its value can be deemed to grow at r per annum.

[3] In the modern economy there is, of course, a wide diversity of government bonds even if we restrict ourselves to long-term issues. We simplify the treatment, for the time being, by assuming there is only one type of long term government bond, say 'perpetuities' – that is, interest-bearing bonds having no redemption date, such as British Consols.

CHAPTER 23

Investment Criteria in a Pefect Economy

1. Investment criteria, whether based on discounted present value or internal rate of return, are devised so as to enable us to choose between alternative uses of investible funds. If there are two or more alternative investment options each has to be compared with the others.[1] If there is only one investment project under consideration, the alternative would be either to use the funds for private expenditures, or for buying government securities. The latter course of action may be thought of as a financial transaction that does not of itself result in any new investment. Initially it is but a purchase of government bonds on the open market: a transfer of funds from the individual to the government. For society as a whole, however, and certainly for public investment, we must transcend all financial transactions and, in the last resort, consider at least two alternatives: either consumption or else investment in this particular project. If there is only one rate of interest on the market, which we are assuming to be the case for the present, it will generally be used as the relevant rate of discount in the present value criterion, *provided* that this market rate reflects society's rate of time preference. A rate of interest of 5 per cent that reflects society's time preference implies that society is indifferent as between $1 today and $1.05 in a year's time. If, therefore, one removes $1 worth of consumption today and returns $1.06 worth of goods next year, society is deemed to gain by the transaction. If, instead, one returns $1.04 in a year's time, society is deemed to be worse off from having postponed consumption. Consequently if a particular investment yields more than 5 per cent in a year's time, society is deemed better off from switching resources from the production of consumption goods to this particular investment good, and vice versa.

In circumstances where the only two alternatives open to the use of

[1] It is just possible that the reader may be wondering why we have continuously ignored mention of depreciation in the treatment of investment criteria. The short answer is that the principles which guide the rate of *amortization* are unrelated to those that arise in *selecting investments*. There is nothing mysterious about this. All investment criteria, whether based on discounted present value or internal rate of return, implicitly make allowance for the maintenance of capital through the requirement that the outlays on the investment project be (more than) covered by the discounted present value of its expected future benefits.

125

present resources are either investment today in a sepcific project or else consumption today, the investment project will be chosen if its internal rate of return exceeds the 5 per cent social rate of time preference. As for the net discounted present value of this investment project, it is sure to be positive (since, by definition of the internal rate of return, the net present value of this investment stream is zero when discounted by a rate *higher* than 5 per cent), and is therefore admissible also on the present value criterion. A positive net present value, given the rate of discount equal to the social rate of time preference, indicates that the present value equivalence of the future benefit stream – as valued by society at its own rate of time preference – exceeds the present value produced by the same resources if, instead, they are used to produce consumption goods. Society is therefore better off by investing these resources and consuming the future products than by consuming their product today. In sum, undertaking *any* investment project that has a higher internal rate of return than the 5 per cent social discount rate, and therefore yields a net present discounted value greater than zero, makes society better off than it would be using the resources instead for present consumption.

2. In an ideal market economy, in which the existing rate of interest reflects the social rate of time preference, the economy is in equilibrium. If this rate of interest is 5 per cent, the marginal product of the existing capital stock is also equal to 5 per cent and, indeed, the internal rate of return on the current volume of investment – the so-called marginal efficiency of investment – is also equal to 5 per cent. In such an ideal economy, at the moment of equilibrium, any new investment opportunity having an internal rate of return above 5 per cent – or a net present value above zero when discounted at 5 per cent – will add to social welfare, as indicated above, and will be undertaken. Such investments will also appear immediately profitable to private persons and corporations. For, in a perfect capital market, they can sell the prospect of the future stream of returns (expected with certainty) for a present value that is larger than the initial outlay. The difference between the initial outlay and the present value so calculated becomes an immediate profit. If the investment stream is −100, 63, 66, the value of the benefits, 63 in year one and 66 in year two, when discounted to the present at 5 per cent discount, is 120. Once these subsequent benefits are assured by spending an initial outlay of 100, he can sell them on the market for a present sum of 120, the difference, 20, being pure profit.

In this long run equilibrium, with social rate of time preference equal to the existing (riskless) rate of return on investment, a straight-forward application of the discounted present value formula, or the internal rate of return formula, as already outlined, will suffice for an investment criterion.

3. If, however, we move from this ideal economy to one where the certain yield on private investment is (for whatever reason) above the social rate of time preference, investment criteria become less simple.

One obvious reason why the rate of return on private investment can be above the social rate of time preference in an otherwise perfectly competitive market is because of the provision made for income tax or corporation tax. If 6 per cent per annum is required to attract the current volume of saving, and all investment income is taxed at, say, 40 per cent, then current investment has to offer the public a gross rate of return of 10 per cent. There will then be a difference of (10 per cent less 6 per cent) or 4 per cent per annum, between the rate of return offered by current investment and the social rate of time preference.

In addition to this obvious reason why the rate of return on investment can be above the social rate of time preference there are others: (a) the market may be out of long-run equilibrium, the short-period rate of return on new investment being above that long-period rate which prevails once people's behaviour has time to adjust; (b) institutional imperfections that can act to raise the costs of attracting savings above the gross rate of return (social rate of time preference *plus* tax provision); (c) external effects of investing for future generations which, if internalized into the market, would lower the gross rate of return required to attract the current volume of savings and so, therefore, the social rate of time preference.[2]

[2] An explanation of (c) is offered in Marglin, 1963(b).

CHAPTER 24

Discounted Present Value versus Internal Rate of Return

1. Consider three alternative investment streams, A, B and C, listed in Table IV.2. The undiscounted net benefit ratio, $(B - K)/K$, where B represents the benefits in the first, and only, benefit period, and K represents the initial capital outlay, would rank C greater than A. Why the *undiscounted* net benefit ratio? Since any rate of discount affects each of the benefits at t_1 in exactly the same proportion, we may infer that whatever the discount rate, the resulting discounted net benefit ratio would give the same ranking as the undiscounted ratio.

This conclusion is valid, however, only for a two-period investment in which the outlay appears in the first period, and the benefit in the second. Add but one more period, and the ranking will in general depend upon the discount rate. For instance a stream $-100, 10, 100$ cannot be ranked with respect to the stream $-100, 90, 10$ without knowing the discount rate. If this were 1 per cent, the first would clearly yield a larger net benefit ratio than the second. If, however, the discount rate were 50 per cent, the second would yield a larger net benefit ratio than the first.

The two-period investment stream also has another property: the ranking of investment streams by their internal rates of return, as shown in the last column of Table IV.2, is equal to the undiscounted net benefit ratio. $(B - K)/K$, and therefore produces the same ranking. There is no mystery about this: the excess benefit, $B - K$, as a fraction of the capital cost, K, is equivalent to one year's growth of the initial capital, K. Thus the capital of 100 in A will have been perceived to grow by 5 per cent, and in C by 25 per cent. A discount rate of that same percent – 5 per cent for A and 25 per cent for C – will therefore reduce the magnitude of the benefit so as to equal the original cost, which result follows the definition of the internal rate of return.

For such two-period investment streams, then, the ranking is unambiguous. Whatever the rate of discount, whether zero or any positive or negative figure, the ranking remains unchanged, and indeed gives exactly the same order as a ranking based on the internal rate of return.

Table IV.2

	t_0	t_1	$(B-K)/K$	Internal rate of return
A	−100	105	$\dfrac{5}{100}$	5%
B	−100	115	$\dfrac{15}{100}$	15%
C	−20	25	$\dfrac{25}{100}$	25%

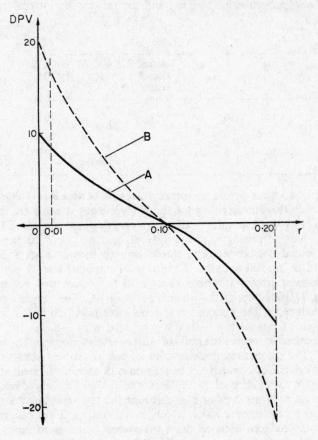

Fig. IV.2

129

2. This harmony between the present value criterion and the internal rate of return criterion will, however, as the reader surely suspects, break down if any of the investment streams being compared contains more than two periods. Indeed, this implication accords with the proposition exemplified above: that for investment streams in excess of two periods the ranking will vary with the rate of discount used. The internal-rate-of-return ranking does not, however, depend on the adopted rate of discount at all, but is independently determined. If it then so happens that, at the ruling discount rate, a number of investment streams show the same ranking by the two criteria, an alteration of the discount rate, which changes the present value ranking of the investment projects, will also produce a discrepancy between this new present-value ranking and the ranking by internal rate of return.

Table IV.3

	t_0	t_1	t_2	Internal rate of return	$(B-K)/K$ at 1%	$(B-K)/K$ at 10%	$(B-K)/K$ at 20%
A	-100	110	0	10%	$\dfrac{9}{100}$	0	$\dfrac{-8}{100}$
B	-100	0	121	10%	$\dfrac{19}{100}$	0	$\dfrac{-16}{100}$

The two three-period investment streams, A and B in Table IV.3, illustrate this simple inference. Both investment streams are ranked equally by the internal rate of return criterion, each yielding 10 per cent. Not surprisingly, if the rate of discount were 10 per cent, discounted net benefit ratio would be zero in each case, and they would be ranked equally. If the rate of discount were 1 per cent, investment stream B would show a higher discounted net benefit ratio, 19/100, compared with that for A, 9/100. The reverse ranking is produced if the discount rate were changed to 20 per cent—B's net benefit ratio being $-16/100$ compared with $-8/100$ for A. A diagrammatic representation of these results appears in Figure IV.2. The discounted present value of the investment streams, and therefore the discounted net benefit ratio of each investment stream A and B, varies inversely with the rate of discount measured horizontally. At a 10 per cent rate of discount the two investment streams have the same present value, which is zero. Since a 10 per cent rate of discount reduces each of these investment streams to zero, their internal rates of return are, by definition, equal to 10%. For discount rates of less than 10 per cent, at which the net present value of both streams are equal,[1] B's present value exceeds that of A, the reverse being true for rates in excess of 10 per cent. ⟩

3. In spite of this discrepancy between the two criteria, the internal rate of return has been recommended in some circumstances, particularly as a method of allocating a given capital budget among a number of potential investment projects. Thus, it has been proposed by McKean (1958) that one select a number of public investment streams, subject to a budget, provided that the internal rate of return on each investment stream that is chosen exceeds the adopted rate of discount. The scheme is illustrated in Table IV.4, which shows five investment streams in declining order of internal rate of return. The discounted net benefit ratio, $PV_r\{(B-K)/K\}$ is also given for a discount rate equal to 3 per cent.

If the capital budget were 1,000 on this selection criterion, only 350 of it would be spent. We should admit A, B, C and D. But we should not admit E. Only the first four projects have an internal rate of return in excess of the 3 per cent discount rate. Project E has an internal rate of return of only 2 per cent, which is below the 3 per cent discount rate.

Table IV.4

	t_0	t_1	t_2	Internal rate of return	$PV_r\{(B-K)/K\}$ (for $r=0.03$)
A	-100	110	0	10%	$\dfrac{7}{100}$
B	-100	0	115	7%	$\dfrac{8}{100}$
C	-100	106	0	6%	$\dfrac{3}{100}$
D	-50	52	0	4%	$\dfrac{1}{100}$
E	-200	2	208	2%	$\dfrac{-2}{200}$

[1] Irving Fisher has defined the term *rate of return over cost* as the discount rate at which the $PV_r\{(B-K)/K\}$ ratio of two alternative investment streams are equal. In general this rate of return over cost is *not* equal to zero, as in the example above, and as depicted in Figure IV.2. The significance of this rate of return over cost figure is simply that of revealing the discount rate at which ranking reversal takes place.

The reader will doubtless observe that the ranking by present discounted value (at 3 per cent) of the four selected investment options differs from the ranking produced by their internal rates of return. But this is no matter, since the same four investment options would be admitted also, and the E project excluded, on either criterion.

If the capital available were only 200, the internal-rate-of-return criterion would select A and B, a choice which would be confirmed by the net benefit ratio. However, let the capital available be only 100, and we are, again, faced with a problem. The internal-rate-of-return criterion chooses the A investment option. The net benefit ratio chooses instead the B investment option.[2] Again, the reader may be inclined to put his faith in the latter criterion. If the rate of discount that is operative is 3 per cent, he will choose the B stream since he can exchange it for a net profit of 8 today, whereas the A stream can be exchanged for a net profit of only 7 today.

4. A further consideration also seems to tell against the use of the internal-rate-of-return criterion: more than a single rate of return may correspond to a given investment stream. A necessary, though not sufficient, condition for more than one internal rate of return to correspond with an investment stream is that not all the costs be incurred in the initial period: there will have to be net disbursements at later periods.

A simple example of such an investment stream, H, would be $-100, 350, -400$, which yields two internal rates of return, λ_1 of 46 per cent, and λ_2 of 456 per cent, since using either of these rates as a discount rate would reduce the present value of this stream to zero, as required by the definition of the internal rate of return.[3]

Figure IV.3, depicts the curve relating the net present value of the H stream to the rate of discount, r. The curve will be seen to cut the horizontal axis, not once (as does each of the investment streams in Figure IV.2), but twice; once at the point where r is 0.46, and once

---

[2] The problem would arise even with a capital budget of 300 or more if the A and B investment streams were *mutually exclusive*, i.e. if, in any list of investment projects, we could include either A or B, but not both.

[3] From the definition of the internal rate of return, say λ, we require a λ for which

$$-100 + \frac{350}{(1+\lambda)} - \frac{400}{(1+\lambda)^2} = 0.$$

The reader will recognize the expression as yielding a quadratic equation with two solutions for λ, 0.46 and 4.56.

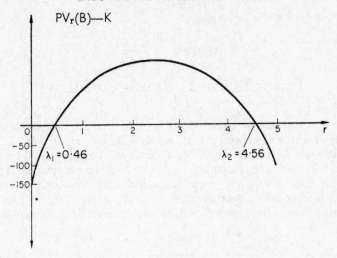

Fig IV.3

where r is 4.56. Since either of these two discount rates reduces the present value of the H stream to zero, they are identified as the two internal rates of return, λ_1 and λ_2.

Of course, the reader might think that of these two internal rates of return, λ_1 (46 per cent) is the more reasonable. If he were obliged to adopt an internal rate of return for such a stream, he would probably choose 46 per cent. But he would find it difficult to justify such a choice. Although 46 per cent might look more reasonable than 456 per cent, his suspicions will surely be aroused[4] when he observes from the figure that for rates of discount *below* 46 per cent, the net present values of the stream are all negative. Indeed, for a zero rate of discount, the net present value is -150. We have, finally, to bear in mind that this two-benefit investment stream is only a special case. For one can devise investment streams to yield three, four, or indeed, any number of internal rates of return. However openminded the reader may wish to remain, he cannot deny that the case for preferring the present-value criterion above the internal-rate-of-return criterion looks very strong.

[4] In fact neither of these rates correspond with the concept of an average rate of growth over time. See Mishan, 1967, for the calculation of an average rate of growth, and for a procedure that reconciles the internal rate of return ranking with that produced by DPV.

CHAPTER 25

Excess Benefit or Benefit-Cost Ratio?

1. If we decide to ignore internal rates of return and to accept only investment criteria based on discounting present values, we would still appear to have three choices. We could rank (1) by net present value, (2) by benefit-cost ratio, or (3) by net benefit-cost ratio. These three alternative investment criteria are compared in Table IV.5 for two investment streams, A and C, where K' is the present value of the outlays, and B' is the present value of the benefits both

Table IV.5

	K'	B'	(1) $B' - K'$	(2) B'/K'	(3) $(B' - K')/K'$
A	100	150	50	1.5	0.5
C	20	50	30	2.5	1.5

discounted, say, at 10 per cent. In the $(B' - K')$ column, A having excess benefit over cost of 50 is ranked above C with an excess benefit over cost of only 30. In the next, B'/K' column, however, C having a ratio of benefit to cost of 2.5 is ranked above A having a ratio of benefit to cost of only 1.5. In the final column showing $(B' - K')/K'$, the ratio of *excess* benefit to cost continues to show C ranked above A. A glance at the last two columns will assure the reader that B'/K' and $(B' - K')/K'$ will give the same ranking, since the latter ratio is derived from the former simply by subtracting unity from it. We can, then, ignore the B'/K' ratio and compare $B' - K'$ with $(B' - K')/K'$.

2. Now if there is a capital budget of exactly 100, it may seem reasonable to be guided by the $(B' - K')/K'$ ratio ranking, and therefore to choose C rather than A. This is rational enough if it is established that he can have either A alone or, instead, five of the C streams. The outlay for five of the C streams uses up exactly the budget of 100, and produces a discounted present value of five times 50, or 250 – which is 100 more than can be got by choosing to invest the budget of 100 in A. But suppose, now, that there is an opportunity for only a single C investment, what then? We should have 80 left over after putting 20 of the capital into C. If we could use this 80 left over in A (the A investment stream being divisible) it would be

better to invest 20 in C and the remaining 80 in A, than to put the whole 100 in A for, in the former case, the present value of the benefits would be $((0.8 \times 150) + 50)$, or 170, while in the latter case the present value of the benefits is only 150. But just as it may not be possible to increase the C investment, the A investment stream may not be divisible. In that case we have a choice—all the A stream, or all the C stream. If there were no other opportunities for the 80 left over from choosing the C stream, we should choose the A investment stream. Even if the funds left over from a choice of C did not have to be returned, but could be used to invest in the private investment sector of the economy at, say, 10 per cent, the A stream would still be chosen. For the adoption of 10 per cent as the discount rate ensures that the outlay of 80 invested in the private sector at 10 per cent per annum in perpetuity has a present value of no more than 80. There is, then, no excess benefit from using the 80 left over in the private sector if C were chosen; the excess benefit resulting from this course of action would still be 30 – just as little as it would be if, instead, the 80 were returned to the government.

It is apparent that, under these conditions, investment stream A should be chosen. And if such conditions did prevail we should use the $(B' - K')$, or excess benefit, method of ranking which would place A, having an excess benefit of 50, above C having an excess benefit of only 30. It is no less apparent that if any multiple of the C investment stream were technically feasible, we should be maximizing the excess benefit of the given capital funds of 100 by opting for C rather than A. Under those conditions, the $(B' - K')/K'$, or excess benefit over cost ratio, method is the correct one to employ. Put differently, if we adopted the $(B' - K')$ method of ranking, we tacitly suppose that the alternative investment streams are of exactly the size given: no increase is possible. If, however, we adopt the $(B' - K')/K'$ method of ranking, we tacitly suppose the opposite; that either stream can be increased in any proportion. Where neither of these suppositions are true, we should not repose confidence in either method of ranking. We should then want to compare the present value of the benefits from using the given 100 of funds in each of the feasible number of ways.

CHAPTER 26

What Should the Rate of Discount Be?

1. Let us set the stage in a competitive full employment economy, one in which, therefore, public expenditure of any kind can be increased only by displacing private expenditure. Let p be the market rate of return on private investment expenditure that is expected with certainty, and let r be the social rate of time preference. If p is equal to r, there is no problem: the discount rate cannot be other than the given numerical value of r or p. If p is greater than r, however, which (for reasons given earlier) is the normal case, the question arises whether to use p or r, or something in between. In general terms, the answer depends upon the alternative opportunities open to the investible funds at the disposal of the public agency, and these opportunities will, in turn, depend upon how the funds are raised and upon the political or administrative constraints that are imposed on the use of these funds.

2. The funds available for public investment can be raised either (a) wholly by reducing current private investment, or (b) wholly by reducing private consumption, or (c) by reducing both private investment and consumption. Consider these three possibilities in turn.

(a) If the government raises, say, $1 million for a public project by borrowing this amount entirely from the market, so reducing current investment in the private sector by $1 million, the value of the annual increment of output that is forgone there is $1 million *times* p. In order then to justify the placing of this $1 million instead in some public investment, it must be expected to earn there an average return of more than p it could have earned in the private sector. If therefore we use p as the discount rate for the public investment stream and we discover that the resulting present value of the benefits exceeds the capital outlay of $1 million, then we are are sure that the investment of $1 million in this public project earns more than it would do in the private sector.

Put otherwise, if $1 million is invested and reinvested in the private sector, it will yield at the end of n years a sum exactly equal to $1 million $(1 + p)^n$. Therefore only if the $1 million, when taken from the private sector and invested in the particular public investment,

136

yields *more* than \$1 million $(1 + p)^n$ at the end of n years is there economic justification for the government agent's borrowing the funds from the private investment sector. But if the \$1 million invested in the public project does yield a terminal benefit in excess of \$1 million $(1 + p)^n$ then, when discounted back to the present at p, its present value will be larger than \$1 million. It follows that only if the present value of the public project's stream of benefits, when discounted at p, exceeds its initial outlay of \$1 million is there economic justification in displacing private investment by this public project.

For the (a) case, at least, p can be regarded as the appropriate rate of discount, and $PV_p(B) > K$ as the appropriate criterion – where $PV_p(B)$ is shorthand for the present value of the stream of benefits when discounted at p, and K is the initial total outlay, here \$1 million.

3. (b) Suppose, instead, that the funds for the public project are now raised wholly by reducing consumption expenditure. Since a reduction of private consumption of \$1 million today has an equivalent *social* value of \$1 million $(1 + r)$ in a year's time, and is equivalent to a social value of \$1 million $(1 + r)^n$ in n years' time, similar reasoning to that in (a) might suggest that in this case the appropriate rate of discount would be r, society's rate of time preference.

But, however the funds are raised, there is always the option of placing the \$1 million (raised by reducing current consumption) in the private investment sector, there to earn \$1 million *times p* in perpetuity. In that case the appropriate rate of discount is again p. Only in the special case where restrictive political or administrative conditions are attached to the use of the funds so raised, will this conclusion be altered. For example if, despite the evident economic irrationality of the condition, the \$1 million raised by reducing consumption is politically tied to a particular public investment, so that if this public investment cannot be justified the \$1 million is not to be raised at all (or if already raised, to be returned to the consuming public), then the yield p in the private investment sector becomes irrelevant. For the \$1 million may not, for political reasons, be invested in the private sector.

In these circumstances the choice lies between consuming the \$1 million this year or investing it only in this particular public project. And clearly, so long as there is this restricted choice, we should choose the public investment project only if it can do better for society: if, that is, it can be made to yield in the public project a sum that is more than \$1 million $(1 + r)^n$ at the end of n years – the sum in n

years time as between which and $1 million today society is deemed to be indifferent. It follows that if discounting the benefit stream of the public project by r yields a present value that is greater than $1 million, we shall indeed do better to adopt the public project than to leave the $1 million to current private consumption.

We conclude that for the (b) case, and whenever there are political constraints restricting the funds raised to particular public projects, the appropriate rate of discount is r, the social rate of time preference.

4.   (c) The final case is that in which a proportion of the $1 million is raised by reducing current consumption, the remainder being raised by reducing current private investment. This may be thought the more general case, for of an increase in taxation of $1 million, a proportion c, equal to the marginal propensity to consume, may result from a reduction in current consumption, the remaining proportion, (1-c), being a reduction of current saving and therefore – given a flexible rate of interest – a reduction in current private investment.

The first thing to be said of such a mixed case is, as already indicated, that *provided* the whole of the $1 million raised has access to the private investment sector, then – irrespective of how the $1 million is raised – its use in any particular public project(s) entails a sacrifice of p *times* $1 million per annum. It follows that the appropriate discount rate (where there are no constraints on investment options) will be p.[1]

If, however, political constraints are so introduced as to confine the $1 million so raised to the particular public project(s), we have again to compare the alternative uses to which the $1 million may be put, failing its use in the public project(s). The principle to be followed is easily illustrated by an example in which p is 10 per cent per annum, r is 5 per cent per annum, and 80 per cent of the $1 million raised by taxation entails a reduction of current consumption.

If we assume that the whole of any returns to the private investment sector is reinvested at 10 per cent then every dollar that is displaced from the private sector would have yielded $0.2 (1 + 0.1)^n$ from the 20 cents invested and $0.8 (1 + 0.05)^n$ from the 80 cents consumed. Since their sum can be equated to $(1 + p')^n$, the appropriate discount rate is p'. If, for example, n is equal to 2, this sum becomes $0.2 (1.1)^2 + 0.8 (1.05)^2$, a terminal value of 1.124 or, approximately $(1 + 0.06)^2$, and 6 per cent therefore becomes the appropriate rate of discount.[2]

---

[1]   See Mishan, 1967.

[2]   Cf. Marglin, 1963(a) for an alternative procedure.

5. Before ending the chapter there are two further considerations which may require modification of the above conclusions.

The first is the common assumption that a proportion of the returns in any year from private investment is used for consumption purposes, the remainder being reinvested. Thus an additional \$1 million in the private investment sector does *not* become \$1 million $(1 + p)^n$ after n years, but a sum less than this since, of each dollar return at the end of each year, only a proportion is reinvested to produce an increment p the following year.[3] This behaviour is not irrational for the *individual* if he takes p to be equal to his personal rate of time preference. But it would be irrational for *society* to adopt this behaviour since the value of any additional dollar consumed today is socially equivalent only to an additional \$1.05 next year, whereas withdrawing this dollar from investment entails a loss of \$1.10 next year. But whether this behaviour of private investors is rational or irrational, it does not necessarily enter into the calculation of public investments. For in the *absence* of constraints on the investible funds available to public agents, the alternative to using such funds for public investment is *not* that of returning them to private investors (the terminal sum being then dependent upon the proportion of the annual return they consume). The superior alternative is that of placing these funds directly in the private sector and, by wholly reinvesting the returns, maximizing the terminal value.[4]

The second consideration relates to the political constraints placed on the consumption of any of the benefits of the public project. As indicated above, wherever p is above r, it would be irrational for any of the returns to public investment to be used for current consumption rather than for reinvestment. If the benefits are indirect, such as cleaner air, water or better health, the government can always transform the value of the benefits into cash returns simply by imposing taxes calculated to produce their value. These tax proceeds can then be wholly reinvested in the private sector at p.

If, however, there are constraints that prevent the public agency acting in this way, some or all of the benefits in any of the years will

[3] The remainder of each dollar of return at the end of the year, being consumed, can be regarded as equivalent in value to $\$(1+r)$ in the following year.

[4] In the *presence* of political constraints, however, the weighted formula for the discount rate requires modification. This is easier to make by compounding forward to the nth period the amount the \$1 million would have become if it had been left to the consumption and investment pattern of the private sector, and comparing this terminal sum directly with the alternative terminal sum if the \$1 million had been invested in the particular public project. The method of compounding forward to terminal sums that are ranked directly is elaborated in Mishan, 1967.

be effectively consumed as they occur. Since a dollar consumed in year t is socially equivalent to consumption of $\$1(1 + r)$ in the following year, and $\$1(1 + r)^2$ the year after, it should be clear that any amount of the tth benefit consumed at time t has to be compounded forward to the end of the terminal period, say n years, at the rate r. The sum of such terminal values so compounded is then to be discounted to the present at the appropriate discount rate p.[5]

References and Bibliography for Part IV

Alchian, A., 'The Rate of Interest, Fisher's Rate of Return over Costs, and Keynes' Internal Rate of Return', *American Economic Review*, 1955.

Bailey, M. J., 'Formal Criteria for Investment Decisions', *Journal of Political Economy*, 1959.

Eckstein, O., 'Investment Criteria for Economic Development', *Quarterly Journal of Economics*, 1957.

———— 'A Survey of the Theory of Public Investment Criteria', in *Public Finances, Needs, Sources and Utilization*, London: National Bureau of Economic Research, 1961.

———— *Water Resources Development – the Economics of Project Evaluation*, Cambridge, Mass: Harvard University Press, 1958.

Galenson, W. and Liebenstein, H., 'Investment Criteria, Productivity and Economic Development', *Quarterly Journal of Economics*, 1955.

Hirshliefer, J., 'Theory of Optimal Investment Decision', *Journal of Political Economy*, 1958.

Lorie, J. and Savage, L. J., 'Three Problems in Rationing Capital', *Journal of Business*, 1955.

Marglin, S., 'The Opportunity Costs of Public Investment', *Quarterly Journal of Economics*, 1963 (a).

———— 'The Social Rate of Discount and the Optimal Rate of Investment', *Quarterly Journal of Economics*, 1963(b).

Margolis, J., 'The Economic Evaluation of Federal Water Resource Development', *American Economic Review*, 1959.

McKean, R. N., *Efficiency of Government Through Systems Analysis*, London: Wiley, 1958.

Mishan, E. J., 'A Normalization Procedure for Public Investment Criteria', *Economic Journal*, 1967.

Robinson, R., 'The Rate of Interest, Fisher's Rate of Return over Costs, and Keynes' Internal Rate of Return: Comment', *American Economic Review*, 1956.

Solomon, E., 'The Arithmetic of Capital-budgeting Decisions', *Journal of Business*, 1956.

Steiner, P. O., 'Choosing among Alternative Public Investments in the Water Resources Field', *American Economic Review*, 1959.

Usher, Dan, 'The Social Rate of Discount and the Optimal Rate of Investment: Comment', *Quarterly Journal of Economics*, 1964.

[5] This device is equivalent to the method of compounding forward to terminal period, n, all the *reinvestible* parts of the benefits at the rate p, and all the *consumed* parts of the benefits at rate r, the resulting aggregate being discounted to the present at the appropriate rate of discount.

CHAPTER 27

Popular Methods of Coping with Uncertainty

1. In evaluating any investment project there is sure to be some uncertainty about the future stream of costs and benefits. Changes in tastes, discoveries of new sources of supply, and technological innovations, all act over time to raise or lower the prices of goods produced by, and inputs used by, the project in question, in ways we may sometimes guess at but cannot foresee.

The distinction frequently made between risk and uncertainty, though not a hard one, does illuminate the problem. Insurance companies cannot say in advance what is going to happen to a particular person. But from the experience of the past, based on large numbers of people, they are able to predict within a small margin of error just how many persons out of every thousand in a certain age group and occupation will, say, fall ill of a certain disease, or have a certain type of accident, within the year. This kind of knowledge enables them to set the insurance premiums at levels high enough to cover all expected claims and offset all the expenses incidental to managing the insurance business. More generally, insurance companies base their calculations on probability distributions that are deemed to alter only slowly over time.

In contrast, uncertainty can be defined as arising from complete ignorance of the relevant probability distribution. But just as knowledge of the required probability distribution is seldom certain, so also is the ignorance implied by uncertainty seldom complete. Thus, although we may be unable to talk with any assurance of the likelihood of any particular event (such as the existence of a particular price) prevailing three years hence, we might be able to bet that it will fall within some range. We may feel fairly confident that it will never assume magnitudes above or below what we should regard as extreme values.

We may note in passing that the optimal size or structure of an investment project may also require knowledge of probability distributions other than those of prices of inputs or outputs. The optimal size of a reservoir or dam, for instance, will depend on the probability of flood damage in the future, which distribution will be based on records going back forty, fifty, or more years. But aside from the need for such probability distributions in order to determine the optimal size or structure of the investment project, we shall also have to have some idea of the movement of prices over time if we are to evaluate the excess benefits of any such project.

2. Of the several methods for dealing with future uncertainty that are discussed in the economic literature, only four are in common use in evaluating investment projects.[1]

(a) The crudest way of dealing with uncertainty is that of adopting a cut-off period. In the case of very risky projects, and as indicated in Chapter 21, this may be as short as three or four years. This means that unless capital is expected to be wholly recouped within three or four years, such an investment is not undertaken. For public investment, however, the cut-off period is appreciably longer and, indeed, can range from thirty to fifty years.

The cut-off period is sometimes supplemented by one of the other methods, either (b) the arbitrary adding of a premium – say one or two per cent to the otherwise appropriate rate of discount – or else (c) the downward revision of expected future output prices and the upward revision of expected future input prices.

Another method (d) is that of introducing 'subjective probability' into the calculation. It has been recommended as an essential procedure in the investment decisions of large corporations,[2] and also as a device appropriate for investment decisions in poor countries, especially in those where the amount of public investment undertaken is not large.[3] Risk and uncertainty is allowed for simply by estimating or, more truthfully, guessing – in addition to the *most likely* future price of each input and output – both an upper and a lower limit to it. In this way a triple of cost-benefit estimates can be produced: a most likely, and, in addition, a most optimistic and a most pessimistic estimate of the excess benefit. Although this is better than depending upon a single most likely estimate, the triple of estimates has the distinct disadvantage that the chance of the most likely estimate occurring can turn out to be very small.

---

[1] Those methods mentioned, but seldom used, in cost-benefit analyses include certainty equivalent, game theory, and utility theory. They are briefly described in my 1971 book.

[2] For example, see D. Hertz (1964).

[3] See S. Reutlinger (1970).

The deficiency of this method can be readily appreciated by an extremely simplified example of a project in which there are no more than four future prices about which there is any uncertainty; say, they are the input prices of a specific grade of iron ore in years 1 and 2, and the output prices of a specific type of steel tubing in years 1 and 2. To simplify further, suppose that the most likely price in each of the four cases is reckoned to have a 60 per cent chance of occurring. The most likely estimate of the excess benefit of the project (whatever it happens to be), that which corresponds to the four most likely prices, will have only a $(0.6)^4$ or, roughly, a 13 per cent chance of occurring. As for the most optimistic and the most pessimistic estimates, each will have a much smaller than 13 per cent chance of occurring. For example, if there is a 20 per cent chance of each of the four most optimistic prices occurring there will be a $(0.2)^4$, or a 1.6 per cent chance, of all four most optimistic prices occurring and, therefore, of the most optimistic excess benefit estimate occurring. Similarly for the most pessimistic estimate. Ordinary prudence would suggest that we discover more about the chances of other possible outcomes before reaching a decision on whether or not to undertake the investment.

3.   A more thorough exploitation of the informed guesses is possible by attaching to each of these three outcomes – the most likely, the most optimistic, and the most pessimistic – of each of the four prices the conjectured probability of its occurring. Since each of the four prices has three alternative estimates, there will be altogether $(3)^4$, or 81, possible excess benefit outcomes[4], each having a distinct chance, or 'subjective probability' of its occurring. One of these 81 possible outcomes, for example, would consist of the most likely input price in year 1, the most optimistic output price in year 1, the most pessimistic input price in year 2, and the most optimistic output price in year 2. If, following the above example, we attach a 60 per cent chance to the most likely price (whether of an input or an output) in periods 1 and 2, and a 20 per cent chance to the most optimistic or pessimistic price (whether of an input or output) in periods 1 or 2, then this particular outcome would have a chance of $(0.6 \times 0.2 \times 0.2 \times 0.2)$, or a 4.8 per cent chance of occurring. In a like manner we could calculate the chance of each of the remaining alternative 80 outcomes occurring.

The resulting probability table cannot, of course, be any more accurate than the subjective estimates of the experts on which they

---

4   For simplicity it is assumed that the movement of each price is independent of that of any other price. If not, there will be fewer than 81 outcomes.

are based. But it does bring out the full implications of these estimates or conjectures, and enables us to say much more than before. By calculating the mean and standard deviation of such a 'probability distribution' of some hypothetical project,[5] we should be able to say, for example, that there is a 90 per cent chance of the excess benefit falling between $150,000 and $250,000, that there is only a $2\frac{1}{2}$ per cent chance of the excess benefit being zero or less, and so on.

In the real world there will, of course, be far more than four uncertain future magnitudes, and it will sometimes be possible to have more than three different estimates for each or some of them. All possible excess benefit outcomes of a single project might then run into millions or hundreds of millions. Nonetheless, with the aid of a computer a sample distribution can be simulated from which the required information can be extracted. The computer is set to select at random one magnitude from the alternative magnitudes attributed to each of the future prices, and from the resulting combination of magnitudes to compute the corresponding excess benefit figure along with the chance of its occurring. A run of 200 or 300 'observations' is usually enough to provide a sample that is reliable enough to work with.

[5] These subjective probability distributions are almost certain to have a normal shape.

CHAPTER 28

The Discount Rate Again

1. For Western economies, where governments invest heavily, there is less need to calculate this sort of subjective probability distribution for the particular project in question. Provided that the risks run by each particular type of private investment are conceived as a probability distribution, the expected, or actuarial, rate of return on the different types of private investment can be regarded as opportunity yields open to the investible funds at the disposal of government agencies. Although the risk of failure is rated higher by the private investor or firm than it is by the central government, or rather by the taxpayers or public at large on whose behalf public investment is made, this fact is not relevant in all circumstances.[1] Certainly, if the funds raised for public projects can always be invested in private industry, some loss is suffered by society in investing the funds in public projects at a lower expected rate of return.

Obviously, the riskier the type of private investment the higher is the expected rate of return—a consequence both of risk-aversion and tax disadvantages under the existing fiscal systems. But whatever the reasons for the higher gross rates of return expected on riskier private investments, they do not weaken the argument. If the placing of public funds in the riskier type of private investment can, in fact, realize these higher gross returns over time, then no public investment should be undertaken that is expected to yield gross returns that are any lower.

To illustrate, if the A-type of private investment has an expected yield of 10 per cent before tax and the B-type of investment, which is riskier, has an expected yield of 14 per cent before tax, then for society as a whole the A-type investment produces a virtually risk-free

---

[1] Arrow and Lind have recently (1970) argued that since the risk run by private investors is larger than that run by taxpayers – which risk approaches zero as their numbers increase – then every one can be made better off, even though public investments are undertaken that yield somewhat less than do private investments. This is held to be possible simply because private investors are prepared to exchange the (risky) rate of return for a *certain* rate of return that is lower than the expected rate of return on public investments. However, the implication, that public investment be undertaken at a lower expected yield than private investment, is valid only if public funds are restricted to particular projects.

return of 10 per cent and the B-type investment produces a virtually risk-free return of 14 per cent. If a particular type of government investment is undertaken that is expected to yield 12 per cent, then the government is forgoing the opportunity of earning, on the average, an additional 2 per cent. Of course, if it were somehow possible to know in advance what each forgone B-type of investment would individually come to, whether 6 per cent or 10 per cent or 18 per cent, then, indeed, that 6 per cent or 10 per cent or 18 per cent would have to be adopted by the government as the actual opportunity rate since this would be the actual yield which could be got by investing in the B-type project. But in fact we do *not* know what each potential B-type private investment will come to yield. We only know that when a large number of a particular B-type private investment are undertaken, their *average* yield is expected to be 14 per cent. If so, public investment is justified only if its own *average* rate of return is expected to exceed 14 per cent—and this is so whether public investment displaces an equal amount of such private investment, or whether the funds are raised by displacing private consumption, or *any* current expenditure, and are not politically restricted to specific investment projects. This requirement can be met simply by using a discount rate of 14 per cent, the average expected return on the highest yielding private investment, and adopting the criterion that the discounted present value of the investment stream be positive.[2]

Finally, if it is a question of an unusually large public investment, involving say $500 million, the alternatives would include that of distributing this amount among a large number of high-risk private investments, from which alternative ones could virtually be certain of earning something close to their average rate of return. In that case we should have to compare the probability distribution of the outcomes of the large public investment with an average of the expected rates of return yielded by the private investments.

References and Bibliography for Part V

Baumol, W. J., 'On the Social Rate of Discount', *American Economic Review*, September 1968.
Carter, C. F. and others (eds), *Uncertainty and Business Decisions*, Liverpool: University Press, 1957.

[2] If, on the other hand, the amount of public investment is very limited, it is in principle appropriate to employ as 'opportunity cost' the whole of the probability distribution of the B-type investment, comparing it with the probability distribution of the outcomes of the public investments in question. In such instances we are directly comparing probability distributions of alternative investment options.

Dorfman, R., 'Basic Economic and Technological Concepts', in A. Maass and others, *Design of Water Resource Systems*, London: Macmillan, 1962.

Friedman, M. and Savage, L. J., 'The Utility Analysis of Choices Involving Risk', *Journal of Political Economy*, 1948.

Hertz, D. B., 'Risk Analysis in Capital Investment', *Harvard Business Review*, Jan./Feb. 1964.

Luce, R. D. and Raifa, H., *Games and Decisions; Introduction to Critical Survey*, London: Wiley, 1957.

Mishan, E. J., *Cost-Benefit Analysis*, London: Allen and Unwin, 1971.

Reutlinger, S., *Techniques for Project Appraisal Under Uncertainty* (World Bank Staff Paper No. 10), Baltimore: John Hopkins Press, 1970.

Schlaiffer, R., *Introduction to Statistics for Business Decisions*, London: McGraw-Hill, 1961.

Shackle, G. L. S., *Expectations in Economics*, Cambridge: University Press, 1949.

Williams, J. D., *The Compleat Strategyst*, London: McGraw-Hill, 1966.

INDEX

accidents and death, evaluating 101–8
accounting prices: of exports, calculating 77; of imports, calculating 73
advertising 44
advertising agency 45
Asia, small holdings 55

benefit: excess, ranking of investment streams by 134; growth induced 37
benefit-cost ratio, ranking of investment streams by 134
bounties 64
bridge: additional, evaluation of 38; evalutation of 37

calculations in cost-benefit analysis 15
capital, normal return on 51
capital expenditure: additional benefits 38; and number of goods in economy 51
compensating variation 14, 96
compensation and hardship 24
consumers and producers, evaluation of 18
consumers' surplus 18; adding and subtracting 32–6; interpretation of 25; measuring 25–31; measuring, inequality factors 37–45; on electricity 34, 41; on gas 34, 41; workable definition 26
contingency calculations 109
cost: economic, of unemployed factors 53–60; marginal 82; marginal, rule 98; rate of return over, definition 131
cost-benefit analysis: limitations 13; reasons for 11–13
cost-difference benefit, evaluation 28
cost pricing marginal 83
cost-saving 25
cost-saving benefit, evaluation 28
counting, double 66–8
Crusoe economy 119
currency, exchange rates 70

data collecting, questionnaire method 110

death: and accidents, evaluating 101–8; gross output approach 101, 102; net output approach 101, 102; risk of, calculating 106; risk of, deficiencies of information 107; see also life, loss of
demand, changes in, and investment 42
demand curve: and income effects 30; and price reductions 32
discount rate 119. 122, 136–40, 145
discounted present value 117, 118–24; excess over cost 120; net 120; versus internal rate of return 128–33
distribution: and equity 22; and prices, equilibrium system 87
domestic economy and foreign trade 74
double counting 66–8

earnings, future, loss of 102
ecology 86
economic analysis, partial 32
economic change, effects 14
economic growth 37
economic production of goods 12
economy 11; number of goods in, and capital expenditure 51; perfect, investment criteria in 125–7
electricity: consumers' surplus on 34, 41; demand curve 41; introduction into all-gas economy 40
environomental spillovers 94
equity 21–4; and distribution 22
errors in counting 66
evaluation, consistency in 18–20
expenditure, additional, multiplier effects 56
exports: accounting prices of, calculating 77; and foreign payments 76
external effects 85–90; definition 86; evaluating 96–100; examples 86, 89, internalizing 91–5; of factory output 92; of noise on economy 88

factory output, external effects 92
flyover, cost-benefit analysis 28
foreign exchange 71

148